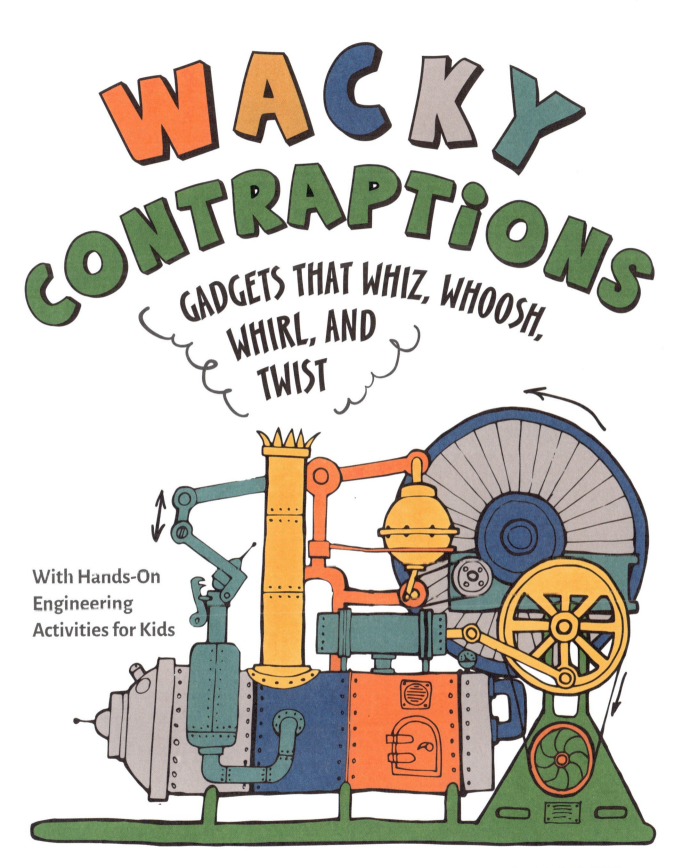

WACKY CONTRAPTIONS

GADGETS THAT WHIZ, WHOOSH, WHIRL, AND TWIST

With Hands-On Engineering Activities for Kids

LAURA PERDEW
Illustrated by Micah Rauch

More engineering titles from Nomad Press

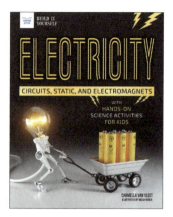 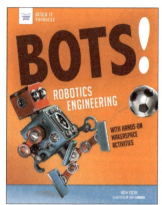 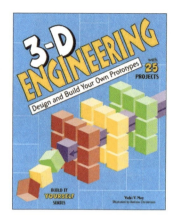 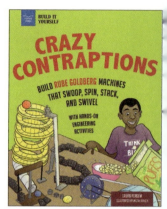

Check out more titles at www.nomadpress.net

Nomad Press

A division of Nomad Communications

10 9 8 7 6 5 4 3 2 1

Copyright © 2025 by Nomad Press. All rights reserved.

No part of this book may be reproduced in any form without permission in writing from the publisher, except by a reviewer who may quote brief passages in a review or **for limited educational use**. The trademark "Nomad Press" and the Nomad Press logo are trademarks of Nomad Communications, Inc.

This book was manufactured by Versa Press, East Peoria, Illinois 978-1-64741-143-5
September 2025, Job #J25-04634
ISBN Softcover: 978-1-64741-143-5
ISBN Hardcover: 978-1-64741-140-4

Educational Consultant, Marla Conn

Questions regarding the ordering of this book should be addressed to
Nomad Press
PO Box 1036, Norwich, VT 05055
www.nomadpress.net

Printed in the United States

CONTENTS

Introduction
Engineering at Play . . . 1

Chapter 1
Tension Time . . . 14

Chapter 2
Amazing Magnets . . . 28

Chapter 3
Get Going with Gears . . . 44

Chapter 4
What's Up with Water? . . . 58

Chapter 5
Mad About Motors, Batteries,
& Electricity . . . 72

Chapter 6
Counting on Chemical Reactions . . . 88

Glossary

Resources

Selected Bibliography

Metric Conversions

Essential Questions

Index

Interested in primary sources? Look for this icon.

Some of the QR codes in this book link to primary sources that offer firsthand information about the topic. Many photos are considered primary sources because a photograph takes a picture at the moment something happens—but watch out for fake ones! Use a smartphone or tablet to scan the QR code and explore more! You can find a list of the URLs in the Resources section. You can also use the suggested keywords to find other helpful sources.

🔎 engineering contraptions

SIMPLE MACHINES

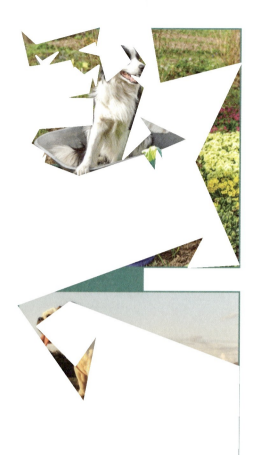

Lever

A rigid bar or arm that pivots on a point called a fulcrum. It is used to move, launch, or lift an object.

Contraption Ideas:
Dominoes, catapult, popsicle sticks, pencils, seesaw

Inclined Plane

A sloped surface used to move an object up or down.

Contraption Ideas:
Book, racetrack, piece of cardboard, train track, ruler, toilet paper or paper towel tube, cereal box

Wheel and Axle

A wheel and a rod that rotate together when force is applied to one or the other. It is used to move objects.

Contraption Ideas:
Toy cars and trains, wheeled cart, built car

SIMPLE MACHINES

Pulley

A wheel with a grooved rim that guides a rope or chain to lift, lower, or move a load.

Contraption Ideas:
Pulley, zip line, rope slung over a fixed bar, rope threaded through a hook

Screw

An inclined plane wrapped around a central axis. It is used to lift and lower objects or hold them together.

Contraption Ideas:
Screw, spiral marble run, spiral slide, flexible tubing wrapped around a central axis, funnel, swirly straws

Wedge

An object that is thick at one end and narrows to a thin edge at the other, used to split, tighten, and lift objects.

Contraption Ideas:
Crafted wedge, doorstop, triangular-shaped blocks and other objects, thumb tacks, nails

Introduction

ENGINEERING
AT PLAY

Is one of your chores at home to water the plants? Many people would fill the watering can and go straight to the plants to water them. Task completed in two simple steps!

But—maybe you find chores boring. Why not add a little fun? Instead of completing the task in two simple (and boring) steps, you could make the whole process way more complicated and ridiculous. In fact, you could create a whole **contraption** just to water the plants.

If that sounds like fun, you are in the right place. This book is all about creating contraptions that involve a series of **chain reactions** to accomplish simple tasks in complex ways.

ESSENTIAL QUESTION

How does designing and building wacky contraptions use engineering principles?

WACKY CONTRAPTIONS

WORDS TO KNOW

contraption: a machine or device that may seem unnecessarily complicated or strange.

chain reaction: a series of events in which one action causes the next one and so on.

engineer: a person who uses science, math, and creativity to design and build things.

engineering design process: the series of steps that guides engineering teams as they solve problems.

brainstorm: to think creatively and without judgment, often in a group of people.

physics: the science of how matter and energy work together.

matter: any material or substance that has **mass** and takes up space.

mass: the amount of matter or stuff in something. On Earth, the mass of something is very close to its weight.

energy: the ability to do work or cause change.

gravity: a force that pulls objects toward each other and all objects to the earth.

force: a push or pull that has the potential to change an object's motion.

Watch this PBS DIY *Science Time* **video to learn more about Newton's laws of motion.** How do Newton's laws apply to seat belts? How does the mass of an object affect its acceleration?

🔎 PBS *Science Time* Newton

THE ENGINEERING DESIGN PROCESS

To build wacky contraptions, it's helpful to know how **engineers** go about designing and building things. Engineers use the **engineering design process** to plan and develop projects. Here are the steps in the engineering design process.

- Identify a challenge
- **Brainstorm** possible solutions
- Draw a plan
- Build the project
- Test it
- Evaluate it
- Redesign the project as needed

When building your contraptions, you will use the engineering design process, too. This will help you learn to think like an engineer. Plus, you'll discover how each step in the process leads to a better contraption.

FEEL THE FORCE

When building contraptions, you need to know a little bit about **physics**, **matter**, and **energy**, including how and why objects move.

ENGINEERING AT PLAY

For that, we turn to an Englishman man named Sir Isaac Newton, who lived hundreds of years ago (1643–1727). Newton made a lot of contributions to mathematics and physics. He's the one who discovered **gravity**. Technically, gravity was always around—Newton just identified it and figured out how it worked.

A portrait of Sir Isaac Newton
Credit: Godfrey Kneller

Another contribution was his three laws of motion. Newton's laws of motion explain the relationships between objects and the **forces** that act on them. A force is a push or pull on an object. That's what keeps an object in one place, moves it, speeds up its movement, slows it down, changes its shape, or changes its direction.

According to legend, Newton developed his theory of gravity after he observed an apple falling from a tree in the mid-1600s. He wondered why the apple moved straight downward instead of upward or sideways.

To better understand how forces work, think about a hockey stick. The stick is used to apply force to slow, stop, or increase the speed of a puck. Often, it's used to change the direction in which the puck travels. Straight into the net!

Forces are all around us, even if we can't see them. What keeps everything from floating away? Gravity! Gravity is a force that pulls objects toward the earth.

WACKY CONTRAPTIONS

> **WORDS TO KNOW**
>
> **friction:** a force that slows a moving object or objects when they move against each other.
>
> **tension:** a pulling force that pulls or stretches an object.
>
> **spring force:** a restoring force found in elastic materials that makes the material stretch or compress and then return to its original position when released.
>
> **electrical force:** the push or pull between two electrically charged objects.
>
> **magnetic force:** a force that occurs when the poles of a **magnet** interact.
>
> **magnet:** a special kind of rock or metal that attracts certain metals.
>
> **air resistance:** the force of air pushing against an object.
>
> **momentum:** a measure of a mass in motion.

Friction, **tension**, and **spring force** are examples of forces, as are **electrical** and **magnetic forces**. We'll explore all of these throughout this book.

Are you wondering why you need to know physics in order to build contraptions? Because you will need to understand how forces impact the objects in your contraption to maintain the chain reaction. This understanding will guide you as you design and redesign your contraptions.

FIRST LAW OF MOTION

Back to Sir Isaac and his three laws of motion. The first law of motion states that an object in motion will stay in motion (moving in the same direction and at the same speed) unless some force acts on it, and an object at rest will stay at rest for the same reason.

But an object doesn't just keep moving forever and ever. Why? Forces! To better understand this, go get a ball of some kind—it doesn't matter what size. Now, roll it along the floor. Eventually, it stops moving, doesn't it? That's because a force (or two) has acted on it.

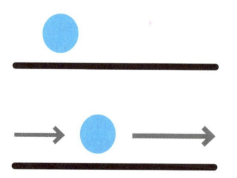

NEWTON'S FIRST LAW OF MOTION
An object in motion will stay in motion.
An object at rest will stay at rest.

Engineering Design Process

Every engineer keeps a notebook to record their ideas and their steps in the engineering design process. As you read through this book and do the activities, keep track of your observations, data, and designs in a design worksheet, like the one shown here. When doing an activity, remember there is no right answer or right way to approach a project. Be creative and have fun!

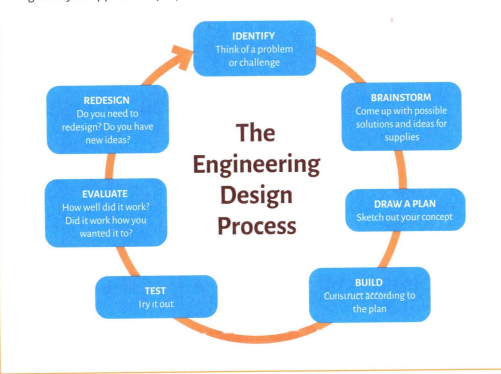

Air resistance is dragging on your ball, slowing its **momentum**. Friction acts on your ball, too. Friction occurs when two objects move against each other. In this case, the ball and floor are in contact, creating friction and slowing the ball.

If you had thrown the ball, there would be forces at work then, too—gravity and air resistance. It might seem hard to believe because air is invisible, but air does cause friction as an object moves through it.

WACKY CONTRAPTIONS

WORDS TO KNOW

newton (N): the unit used to measure force.

input force: the force applied to make an object move.

convoluted: complex and difficult to follow.

exert: to put forth effort or force.

Now, unless you go fetch that ball, it will stay where it landed. That's the second part of the first law of motion. The ball will not move again unless another force acts on it. Maybe that force will be you or your friend or your sibling. Perhaps the neighborhood dog will come along and get that ball moving. You get the idea.

Forces are measured in units called newtons (N), named after Sir Isaac.

SECOND LAW OF MOTION

Newton's second law of motion states that a push or pull on an object will change its speed—how quickly it moves. Plus, the amount of force needed to increase the speed of an object depends on its mass.

To demonstrate this second law, grab your ball again. Give it a little push. That small **input force** will move it slowly a short distance. Now, give the ball a bigger push. The larger input force moves the ball faster across a longer distance.

Let's think about the second part of this second law. An object with more mass, such as a bowling ball, is harder to get moving. It is also harder to slow down. On the other hand, an object with less mass, such as a wiffle ball, requires less force to get it moving or to slow it down.

NEWTON'S SECOND LAW OF MOTION
A push or pull on an object will change its speed.

ENGINEERING AT PLAY

Who was Rube Goldberg?

Rube Goldberg (1883–1970) was an engineer and cartoonist. He became famous during the early 1900s for the cartoon drawings he made of ridiculous, **convoluted** contraptions. These contraptions accomplished simple tasks in overly complicated ways. One of his most famous contraptions was a self-operating napkin. He also invented a simple fly swatter, an automatic sheet music turner, a painless tooth-pulling device, and many others.

Each step in Goldberg's drawings of chain reactions was lettered so people could follow the sequence of events. In addition, he included unusual parts in his contraptions, including rockets, fire, catapults, animals, springs, and pendulums. Goldberg never actually built any of his contraptions, but they were based on real engineering concepts and were designed to actually work if built. His real goal, though, was to make people laugh.

Visit the website of the Rube Goldberg Institute to learn more about Goldberg, the contraptions he designed, and ongoing design competitions. Why do you think Rube Goldberg contraptions are so popular?

🔎 Rube Goldberg Institute

THIRD LAW OF MOTION

Finally, the third law of motion states that for every action, there's an equal and opposite reaction. It's not always obvious, but forces occur in pairs—the action and the reaction. These two forces are the same size but move in opposite directions.

Grab your ball one more time. Go outside with it. Now, give it a kick. Your foot **exerts** an action force on the ball. At the same time, the ball exerts an equal and opposite reaction force on your foot. Feel it?

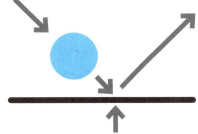

NEWTON'S THIRD LAW OF MOTION
For every action, there's an equal and opposite reaction.

7

WACKY CONTRAPTIONS

WORDS TO KNOW

trial and error: trying first one thing, then another and another, until something works.

work: the amount of energy needed to move an object a certain distance.

potential energy: the energy stored inside an object when it is still or at rest.

kinetic energy: the energy an object possesses when it is in motion.

simple machine: a mechanical device that changes the direction or magnitude of a force. The six simple machines are the lever, inclined plane, wheel and axle, pulley, screw, and wedge.

mechanical advantage: the benefit gained by using a machine to do work with less effort.

You can really feel that force sometimes, especially if you've given the ball a good whack. That's also why kickball is played with a light rubber ball. No one wants a reaction force exerted on their foot from a ball with a greater mass. Imagine how you'd feel if you kicked a bowling ball!

All of these laws of motion do not apply just to the ball you're using. They apply to *everything*. For contraption building, you will use these laws of motion to figure out how to get things to slow down, speed up, and change direction.

WORK AND ENERGY

Another important part of contraption building is understanding that chain reactions are the result of energy transfers from one step to the next. This keeps the momentum going. Some of this you will learn firsthand through **trial and error**. That's how all scientists approach tasks—they try and fail, then try again.

Energy is the ability to do **work**. Another way to think about energy is as the force that causes objects to move some distance. How much work is done depends on how much force is used and over what distance.

WORK = FORCE x DISTANCE

Believe it or not, building contraptions is considered work. According to scientists, anyway! That's because work happens when a force acts on an object and moves it some distance or causes change. All of your building, testing, and redesigning will move many objects.

There are two forms of energy—**potential energy** and **kinetic energy**.

Potential energy is the energy stored in an object due to its position or state. For example, you might include a marble run in one of your contraptions. If you position a marble at the top of the run, it has potential energy because of its position.

Kinetic energy, on the other hand, is energy in action. Once a force has acted on that marble at the top of the run and it's rolling down the ramp, the potential energy converts to kinetic energy. The ball still has the same total amount of energy, it's just in a different form. The energy in your contraptions will transfer from one object to another to create a chain reaction to complete your simple task in a fun and overly complicated way.

SIMPLE MACHINES

Simple machines are the building blocks for contraptions. Each simple machine does one or more of the following: increases the strength of a force, changes the direction of a force, or changes the distance over which you apply a force needed to do work. Simple machines are used to gain what's called **mechanical advantage**.

Rube Goldberg Design Contests

While Goldberg never built any of his contraptions, people around the world do build fun contraptions. There are even design contests! The first was in 1949, when two college students held a contest to see who could build the best contraption.

Now, the Rube Goldberg Institute holds annual competitions. Some are drawing contests and people are invited to design and submit cartoons for their own contraptions. Another is a live event where teams showcase their contraptions designed and built to solve a task. There's an online version of that competition, too, as well as other contests and challenges for contraption-minded people. Schools, universities, clubs, and organizations also hold similar contests for engineers young and old!

WACKY CONTRAPTIONS

This means they make doing work easier because they reduce the amount of force needed to perform a task. Humans have used simple machines for thousands of years! The six simple machines are levers, inclined planes, wheels and axles, pulleys, screws, and wedges. You will learn more about each simple machine in the chapters to come.

Imagination and creativity are key elements when building contraptions!

Engineering Careers

Sure, contraptions are fun to build, but they're also the perfect way to gain skills that could someday help your career. Have you ever thought about being an engineer? Engineers use critical and creative thinking to design everything from office buildings to homes, subway systems to roads, tools to takeout boxes. Takeout boxes? Yes! Packaging engineering is the branch of engineering where people figure out how best to carry stuff!

There are lots of different kinds of jobs in the engineering field. Here are just a few.

› **Mechanical Engineer:** works with mechanical systems such as engines, heating systems, weaponry, and more. These engineers combine physics, math, design, materials, and more to design the systems we rely on.

› **Chemical Engineer:** works in the chemical industry and uses their knowledge of how basic materials can combine into different products to develop new types of fuel, food, and more.

› **Biomedical Engineer:** develops medicines, medical devices, systems, and other solutions so doctors and nurses can better treat and heal sickness and injury.

› **Environmental Engineer:** designs systems that help solve environmental problems to improve air, water, and land quality.

ENGINEERING AT PLAY

Which simple machines can you spot in this wacky contraption?

LET'S GET TO WORK!

Before you get started building your wacky contraptions, keep in mind that you can use supplies you find around the house. Most of the time, you won't need to buy anything. Recycle, reuse, and repurpose things! Look through old toy bins, the recycling bin, and junk drawers for items that will make good building materials. See the resources at the end of this book for more ideas for supplies.

Check out this PBS video to learn more about simple machines and see them in action all around us. What are some examples of simple machines we use in everyday life?

PBS *Science Trek* simple machines

WACKY CONTRAPTIONS

This book has many challenges for you to tackle, but they are just suggestions for being a contraption engineer!

You will likely come up with new ideas for challenges and elements to include in your contraptions. Write down your ideas in your engineering notebook and go for it! You are the engineer here.

Remember to start small. The challenges get bigger and bigger throughout the book. Don't try to do the big ones first. You will learn as you go and your contraptions will grow as you learn. Also, building contraptions can get messy. If you do make a mess, be prepared to clean it up. Always ask for permission to do anything out of the ordinary and to use items that are not yours.

Essential Questions

Each chapter of this book begins with an essential question to help guide your design and creation of wacky contraptions. Keep the question in your mind as you read the chapter. At the end of each chapter, use your engineering notebook to record your thoughts and answers.

ESSENTIAL QUESTION

How does designing and building wacky contraptions use engineering principles?

Keep in mind, many of your contraptions won't work right away. That's okay! If your contraption doesn't work, that's an opportunity to think like an engineer.

Figure out why it doesn't work. Pay attention to parts that did work. Then, redesign and retest.

Be wacky! Be creative! Be complicated! And most importantly, have FUN!

TEXT TO WORLD

What simple machines can you spot in your home or classroom right now? What purpose do they serve?

BALLOONS AND THE LAWS OF MOTION

Newton's laws of motion are at work (and play) all around us every day, yet they may be hard to picture in your mind. It's time to see for yourself how they work! This experiment will help you understand the forces at work when air is released from a balloon.

IDEAS FOR SUPPLIES

- long, skinny balloons
- 10 to 15 feet of string for each balloon
- a straw for each balloon
- tape
- binder or bag clips
- timer

› **For each balloon, thread the string through a straw.** Tape the string to two anchor points, 10 to 15 feet apart and 3 to 5 feet off the ground. Make sure the string it tight.

› **Blow up a balloon about halfway but don't tie it off.** Use large kitchen clips or binder clips to keep the air from escaping.

› **Carefully tape the balloon to the straw on the string.** Pull the balloon back to an anchor point so that the open end of the balloon is closest to the anchor point.

› **Unclip the clip and let go!** Measure and record how far the balloon goes. How was the balloon's movement an example of Newton's third law of motion?

› **Test Newton's second law.** How fast and far the balloon goes depends on how much force is acting on it and the mass of the balloon. Add more force than before by blowing up the balloon more. Does it travel farther? Measure and record how far it goes.

› **Blow up the balloon just a little.** Measure and record how far it travels. Compare the distance the balloon traveled in each of the three trials. What have you discovered about force and the second law of motion?

› **Add mass to your balloon by taping objects to it (coins, popsicle sticks, paper clips).** Test how far the balloon travels with different masses. What have you discovered about mass and the second law of motion?

Super Challenge

Redo this challenge and observe the speed at which the balloon travels depending on the force you apply and the mass of the balloon. Use a timer to measure how fast the balloon moves from one point to another under different circumstances.

Chapter 1

TENSION
TIME

To build your wild and wacky contraptions, you need energy. Energy is what makes things happen. We're not talking about just the energy that you get from eating an apple or a bowl of spaghetti. We're also talking about the energy in your contraptions, which will keep the chain reaction going so you can complete all the overly complicated and ridiculous steps you have designed.

Remember that energy comes in two forms. One is potential energy, which is energy stored in an object that has what it takes to do work. The other is kinetic energy, which is the energy an object has when it's in motion after all that potential energy is released.

> **ESSENTIAL QUESTION**
>
> How can you use the elastic potential energy in springs and rubber bands to do work?

TENSION TIME

Kinetic energy is a bit easier to understand because we can see objects in motion. Potential energy, on the other hand, is trickier. A ball lying on the floor does not appear to have any potential to do anything! But objects do have potential energy.

Sometimes, that potential energy is based on the position of an object. Think of a sled at the top of a snowy hill—gravity will pull the sled down the hill, releasing the sled's potential energy. We'll discuss gravity more later.

Other times, potential energy is based on an object's state. Consider a balloon like the one in the balloon activity in the Introduction. The inflated balloon was full of air. When you released that air, the balloon moved along the string. For objects with potential energy, such as the inflated balloon, that energy is released when the position or state of the object changes.

> **WORDS TO KNOW**
>
> **gravitational potential energy:** the energy stored in an object as the result of its height above Earth.
>
> **vertical:** straight up and down.

GRAVITATIONAL POTENTIAL ENERGY

Think back to Sir Isaac Newton, whom you met in the Introduction. He's the one who developed the theory of gravity and identified gravity as a force. **Gravitational potential energy** is related to an object's **vertical** position, or how high it is off the ground, and its mass. That sled has gravitational potential energy because it's teetering at the top of the hill. When someone gives the sled a push, the force of gravity acts on the sled and potential energy is converted to kinetic energy.

15

WACKY CONTRAPTIONS

WORDS TO KNOW

apex: the highest point of something.

elasticity: the ability of an object or material to return to its original shape after being compressed or stretched.

compress: to squeeze or push a material with force.

stored potential energy: stored energy in an elastic material that results from stretching or compressing.

Have you ever ridden a roller coaster? A roller coaster illustrates gravitational potential energy. At its highest point, the roller coaster has the most potential energy. This potential energy is converted to kinetic energy as the roller coaster races downward on the track.

The conversion of potential energy to kinetic energy is also easy to see when you toss a ball in the air and it reaches its highest point before falling back to the ground. The same thing happens on a swing when you reach the **apex**. Other examples of gravitational potential energy include water held behind a dam, a piece of fruit dangling from a tree, and a marble at the top of a marble run.

You will take advantage of gravitational potential energy in your contraptions throughout the rest of the book!

Track the energy in a moving roller coaster! Watch this simple roller coaster simulation to see where the coaster has potential energy and where that energy converts to kinetic energy. How might this change in energy feel if you were riding that roller coaster?

🔎 PBS roller coaster energy

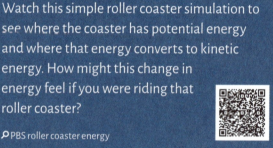

Where is the apex on this roller coaster?

TENSION TIME

ELASTIC POTENTIAL ENERGY

Elasticity is another type of potential energy. This type of potential energy is found in objects such as rubber bands and springs that can be **compressed** or stretched. And the more you compress or stretch an object, the more potential energy it has. It is an excellent type of energy to use in contraptions to get objects moving and to keep the momentum going.

You can create elastic potential energy in your own body—stretch a muscle!

Let's take a closer look at elastic potential energy. Find a rubber band. Stretch it out. The rubber band has **stored potential energy**. Now, let go of one side and let it snap back (but don't stretch it too tightly—the snapping band might sting your hand). When the rubber band snaps back, the potential energy is converted to kinetic energy, which can move an object or sting your hand!

Now, find a clear area where you can shoot the rubber band. Put the rubber band around your index finger on one hand. With the other hand, pull back on the rubber band an inch or so. Aim into an empty room or yard. Never aim toward people or other living things! Release the rubber band with the hand you were pulling with. How far does it fly?

Show Time!

Have you seen the movie *The Goonies*? How about *Home Alone*? These movies make great use of Rube Goldberg machines! Contraptions are fun to build and they're fun to watch on the big screen. Why? Because they combine anticipation with the satisfaction of a smooth chain reaction. Except, of course, when something goes wrong. That's when the movie gets a chance to be funny! You can also find contraptions in *Wallace & Gromit: The Curse of the Were-Rabbit*, *Chitty Chitty Bang Bang*, *Robots*, and *Home Alone II*.

WACKY CONTRAPTIONS

WORDS TO KNOW

patent: the rights granted to an inventor for their invention so others may not copy or take advantage of it.

resistance band: a large elastic band used for strength training.

ricochet: to rebound one or more times off a surface.

catapult: a device used to hurl or launch an object.

battery: a device that produces an electric current using chemicals.

latex: a substance from which rubber can be made, found in more than 2,000 plant species, including rubber trees.

species: a group of living things that are closely related and can produce young.

Mesoamerica: the region that includes parts of Mexico and Central America.

indigenous: native to a certain location or area.

synthetic: produced artificially to imitate a natural product.

fossil fuels: fuel made from the remains of plants and animals that lived millions of years ago. Coal, oil, and natural gas are fossil fuels.

Try shooting the rubber band several times, each time pulling the band back farther and farther. What do you notice?

The farther back you stretch the rubber band before releasing it, the more elastic potential energy it has. The more potential energy the rubber band has, the farther it will fly.

Today, rubber bands are largely used to hold things together. You might also see them as a source of elastic potential energy in gyms in the form of **resistance bands**. Many toy planes and other wind-up toys use rubber bands. And if you were to make a slingshot, you would use a rubber band (look for that challenge later in this chapter).

Rubber bands were patented in 1845 in England and the first rubber band factory opened soon after.

Why is all this knowledge important to contraptions? You could use a rubber band to sling a marble across a table or to wind up a rubber band car. You can also use rubber bands to make an object **ricochet** in a different direction as if in a pinball machine or to create a **catapult** to launch an object. You have many options!

18

TENSION TIME

BOING, BOING, BOING

Elastic potential energy is also found in springs when they are compressed or stretched out. Whether compressed or stretched, when the spring is released, the potential energy is converted to kinetic energy. The more you compress or stretch it, the more potential energy the spring contains.

> **Learn more about the energy contained in springs, including how to use math to measure that energy!** How does this show the relationship between compression and tension?
>
> 🔎 FuseSchool springs

Springs are used in many ways in everyday life. As with rubber bands, they are often used to hold things together—for example, some types of clothespins or clips have springs. Springs can also keep **batteries** tightly in place to ensure they make contact with the electrical terminals. If you have a flashlight or digital kitchen timer, open it up to see the springs and batteries!

The Long History of Rubber

Natural rubber comes from a special substance called **latex**, which is found in more than 2,000 different **species** of plants and trees. One of them is the rubber tree. Humans first used rubber thousands of years ago in **Mesoamerica**. **Indigenous** people there figured out how to harvest the latex and mix it with juices from morning glory vines to shape it and create everyday items. They adapted the process to what they were making. For shoes, the rubber needed to be strong and resist wear. For sports, Mesoamericans wanted their balls to be bouncy. They even made their own form of rubber bands that maximized strength and elasticity.

European explorers to the region during the 1500s had never seen rubber before. They were so fascinated by it that, in addition to gold, they took rubber back to Europe. Today, **synthetic** rubber is made from **fossil fuels**.

WACKY CONTRAPTIONS

WORDS TO KNOW

plasticity: the ability of an object or material to be permanently molded or shaped.

pivot: to turn or move on a fixed spot.

fulcrum: the fixed point on which a lever sits or is supported and on which it moves.

load: something that is carried or moved, especially something heavy.

Some types of equipment combine both gravitational and elastic potential energy for maximum fun—think of spring diving boards and trampolines.

Springs are in some ballpoint pens so you can retract or push out the tip of the pen. Most vehicles have shock absorbers made from springs. Pogo sticks have springs, too, allowing you to jump much higher than you could without them. You might also find springs in garage doors, toys, mattresses, mechanical watches, and certain cameras. Look around. Where else are springs being used?

And, of course, we wouldn't be talking about springs unless they were useful in making contraptions. Like rubber bands, they are an excellent source of energy to set different objects in motion.

Elasticity vs. Plasticity

Elasticity and **plasticity** may seem like similar words, but they're opposites. When objects are pulled, twisted, or pushed, they change shape or become deformed. Elastic objects return to their natural shape after the forces that pull, twist, or push on them stop. Plastic objects stay in their changed form after a force acts on them. We can shape or mold plastic easily, and plastic objects maintain their shape.

Plastic items are part of our everyday lives precisely because they can be molded and shaped. They include straws, water bottles, kitchen utensils, furniture, phone cases, eyeglass parts, storage bins, toys, and more. And while elastic and plastic items are different in some ways, most synthetic elastics and plastics are made from oil, though there are some new types of plastic called bioplastics, which are made from plant material.

Learn more about energy with Energy Ant on the U.S. Energy Administration's Energy Kids website. In addition to elastic energy, what are other forms of energy?

🔍 Energy Ant kids

TENSION TIME

SIMPLE MACHINE #1: LEVER

A lever consists of a rigid bar that **pivots** on a support point called a **fulcrum**. There are three different types of levers, and each makes moving, lifting, or launching an object easier. Examples of levers in everyday life include can openers, windshield wipers, seesaws, and crowbars. Even an object such as a baseball bat or hockey stick is a lever because it allows us to move a ball or puck with much more force.

There are three main types of levers—first-, second-, and third-class levers. The location of the **load**, fulcrum, and effort is different for each type of lever. And each type of lever is used for a different job.

A first-class lever has the fulcrum between the load and the effort. A seesaw is an example. The fulcrum is the stand in the center of the long bar and the people sitting on each end are the load and effort.

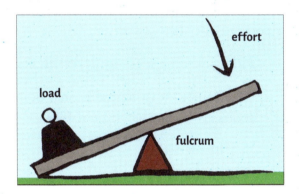

FIRST-CLASS LEVER
The fulcrum is between the load and the effort.

A second-class lever has the load between the fulcrum and the effort. The load moves in the same direction as the effort. A bottle opener is a second-class lever. The fulcrum is where the point of the opener rests on the bottle, and a person applies the effort to wrench off the bottle cap.

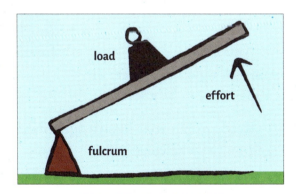

SECOND-CLASS LEVER
The load is between the fulcrum and the effort.

WACKY CONTRAPTIONS

A third-class lever has the effort between the fulcrum and the load. A baseball bat is a third-class lever when you use it to strike a ball.

Levers are very important in contraptions. For example, dominoes can work as levers. How? The fulcrum is the point where the domino sits on a surface. As the domino falls, it moves the next domino or object.

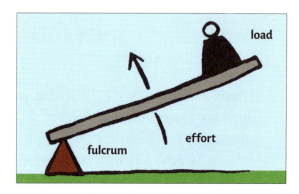

THIRD-CLASS LEVER
The effort is between the load and the fulcrum.

Here are some ideas for levers in contraptions.

- dominoes (can be traditional dominoes or made from cereal boxes, books, wooden blocks, old CD cases, and more)
- popsicle sticks
- Tinker Toys
- Lincoln Logs
- Legos
- rulers
- pencils

Anything that you can use as a rigid bar and set on a fulcrum can be a lever.

Ready to put your knowledge to work and make some contraptions?

Watch the videos of Rube Goldberg machines on the Connecticut Science Center's website to see some very complicated contraptions. How are springs and rubber bands used in these contraptions?

🔍 CT Science Center Goldberg

ESSENTIAL QUESTION

How can you use the elastic potential energy in springs and rubber bands to do work?

TEXT TO WORLD

Look around your home or classroom. Where do you see levers at work? What type are they?

SPRING SPROUTS

Time to add steps and components to your contraption-making. For this challenge, you will make your own springs and also start using dominoes, which are useful in many, many contraptions.

> **Challenge Identified.** Create your own springs to use as the stems for paper flowers. Compress the spring stems and create a two- or three-step contraption to make the flowers "sprout."

> **Brainstorm ideas and supplies.** For the springs, you can use cardboard (a recycled cereal or cracker box works well). For the flowers and leaves, construction paper, pipe cleaners, or paper and markers are all possibilities. You also need an object to hold the spring flower stems compressed until the energy is released. Finally, you need dominoes. Don't have dominoes? What else could you use?

> **Draw a plan.** As you design your contraption, think about how you can both compress the flower stems and then release them. How do the dominoes fit in? You could compress your springs with a dowel and have the dominoes knock the dowel out of place, allowing the flowers to sprout. What will cause the dominoes to fall?

> **Build.** Compressing the stems and keeping them down might take some trial and error. You will learn as you go. That's how many engineering projects work!

> **Test.** When the flowers are ready to sprout, set off your dominoes. Boing!

> **Evaluate.** What did you learn about stored energy in springs? Was it difficult to keep the flowers down? Did the flowers "sprout" as planned? Was there enough force to release the stored energy in the springs?

> **Redesign.** How could you redesign this mini contraption? Maybe use different materials or think of a different way to keep the springs compressed? Redo your drawing and try again!

CONTRAPTION TIP!

Sometimes, engineers and other creators use backward design when planning a project. That means you start with what you want to accomplish. In this case, the goal is to make the flowers spring up. Working backwards, decide how to hold down the springs until it's time for them to release. Next, plan the step before that. Keep thinking backward from there.

DEMOLITION BY **SLINGSHOT**

Let's start with a simple task—demolishing a tower with a slingshot. **In this challenge, you can practice following the engineering design process—from brainstorming and drawing a plan to building, testing, evaluating, and possibly redesigning your contraption.** Not only will you learn to follow the engineering design process, you will also gain experience with the elastic potential energy of rubber bands and get ideas for future contraptions.

> Always be careful when launching objects. Never aim at people or other living creatures.

❯ **Challenge Identified.** Demolition! In this first, very simple contraption, create a slingshot and use it to knock over a tower.

❯ **Brainstorm ideas and supplies.** Obviously, you need a rubber band. What about the base of the slingshot? You can make a simple one with a rubber band, two pushpins (or nails), and a piece of wood. If you don't have any wood, think about other things you could use instead, perhaps several pieces of cardboard glued together or empty toilet paper rolls. How do you want to secure the slingshot to the tabletop? Duct tape? Why do you think you need to secure the slingshot? Next, what can you make the tower out of? Empty toilet paper tubes? Dominoes? Small paper cups? And what kind of object do you want to launch at the tower? A ball? A marshmallow?

❯ **Draw a plan.** Sketch out a plan of this simple contraption. It might look like the drawing below, or it could be totally original.

❯ **Build.** Time to turn your plan into reality!

* Assemble the slingshot by pushing the pins into the piece of wood a couple inches apart. Attach the rubber band to the two pins. You have a slingshot!

* Secure the slingshot to the surface you're using.

* Build the tower—any size you like, but keep in mind that the object you're launching at the tower needs to have enough force to knock over the tower.

> **Test.** Aim the slingshot at the tower and load the object you are launching. Pull back and release the rubber band. Ziiiiing!

> **Evaluate.** Is your tower still standing? Was there too much or not enough force? Did the object launch in the direction you wanted it to? What can you adjust to keep the object on the right path? In addition, did you pull the rubber band back far enough, storing enough potential energy in it to launch the object?

> **Redesign.** Based on your evaluation, redesign your simple slingshot if necessary. You could try using different objects to launch or make the tower smaller or out of something different. The redesign could include "guardrails" to keep your object moving in the right direction. After redesigning, test it again.

CONTRAPTION TIP!

Sometimes, engineers and other creators use backward design during the planning phase of the process. That means starting with what you want to accomplish. In this case, the end goal is to launch the object you've chosen. Working backward, decide how you might hold back the rubber band that will launch it. Next, plan the step before that. Keep thinking backward from there.

Trampolines

If you have ever jumped on a trampoline, you have experienced both elastic and gravitational potential energy firsthand! The trampoline mat itself is like one giant rubber band. And as you jump, gravity is at work.

When you jump up, your gravitational potential energy increases—and the higher you jump, the more potential energy you have. Then, at your highest point, you have a maximum amount of gravitational potential energy. As you begin to fall back toward the trampoline mat, that energy is converted to potential energy.

Also at play (pun intended) is the elastic potential energy of the trampoline. When you land on its surface, the trampoline's springs and mat stretch due to your weight—this stores elastic potential energy. This is then converted to kinetic energy and up you go!

MARSHMALLOW LAUNCHER

For this challenge, explore the elastic potential energy of both a rubber band and a spring. Use what you've learned about elastic potential energy and rubber bands and springs and then add levers to make a marshmallow-launching contraption.

Catapults are a type of lever that you can make with rubber bands. They are great for this type of launching contraption. Once you make the catapult, you will be able to use it again in future contraptions if you want.

> **Challenge Identified.** Create a new contraption that involves three or more steps and that uses a spring. End with a catapult that launches a marshmallow.

> **Brainstorm ideas and supplies.** To make the frame of the catapult, look around your house. You can use popsicle sticks, pencils, toilet paper tubes, straws, empty cans, etc. What can you use for the launching arm? You will need rubber bands, too. Don't forget to include a spring in your contraption. You could make a new one out of cardboard, or search around your house for one. Do you have a Slinky? Some clothespins and clips also have springs in them. What other steps can you add to your contraption to release elastic potential energy and launch the marshmallow?

Heads Up!

Catapults are amazing devices used to hurl or launch an object, such as a water balloon, ball, or pumpkin. Yes, there are actually pumpkin-launching contests held across the United States! You might also use a catapult in your contraption to launch a marshmallow or dog treat.

Yet catapults were historically used for more serious activities. There is evidence that catapults were first used in wartime in ancient China and Greece around 400 **BCE**. They were used to hurl large stones at the enemy and to crumble fortress walls. In other cases, they were used to launch arrows with great force. With time, people made larger and larger catapults to hurl larger and heavier objects. Today, catapults are not used as weapons. However, they are used to launch military planes off an aircraft carrier using a design that is much more advanced than the original.

WORDS TO KNOW

BCE: put after a date, BCE stands for Before Common Era and counts down to zero. CE stands for Common Era and counts up from zero. These non-religious terms correspond to BC and AD.

> **Draw a plan.** There are many types of catapults. Yours may look like this one or it might be simpler or more complicated.

> **Build.** Piece together your catapult, load and get the marshmallow in place.

> **Test.** Ready, aim, fire!

> **Evaluate.** Did the catapult launch the marshmallow? Did it go as far as you'd planned? What parts of the catapult and which steps in the chain reaction do you need to tinker with?

> **Redesign.** Address the parts of the contraption that didn't work like you wanted them to. If the catapult worked fine, you may want to try to launch bigger and better things higher and farther or you may just want to work on its accuracy.

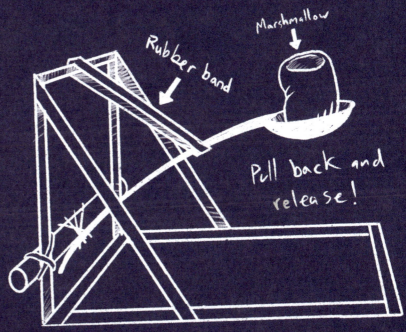

You can make a catapult in many ways using a variety of art supplies and building supplies. Go online to find a design using materials that you already have or check out this link for a more complex project. How does elastic tension make a catapult work?

Instructables desktop catapult

Super Challenge

Consider the many ways you can use rubbers bands and incorporate them into a contraption. Not only can you use rubber bands to fling or toss things forward, you can also use them to hold things together. For example, you could set up rubber bands as bumpers for a ball or marble so it bounces in a new direction. Create a contraption that uses rubber bands in three different ways.

AMAZING MAGNETS

What do you think of when someone mentions magnets? Stuck on the refrigerator door, holding up artwork? Found on the edge of cabinet doors to keep them closed? Classrooms often have magnetic boards where teachers display posters, student work, and assignments. Magnets are marvelous!

ESSENTIAL QUESTION

How can you use the pushing and pulling forces of a magnet to change the direction and speed of a moving object?

A magnet is a material or object that can **attract** other magnets and certain metals, including those made of iron, nickel, and cobalt. Magnets also attract certain types of steel made from iron. A **mineral** called magnetite is attracted to magnets. Magnetite is sometimes naturally magnetic, and then it is known as a **lodestone**.

AMAZING MAGNETS

In addition, the metals that are attracted by magnets can themselves be **magnetized**. Go grab a magnet and a nail or paper clip. If you are using a paper clip, uncurl it to make it semi-straight. Now, rub the magnet along the metal again and again, moving in the same direction each time (not back and forth).

After rubbing the nail or paper clip with the magnet many times, it should act like a magnet. Give it a try. Does your nail or paper clip attract anything made of iron? If it doesn't work, rub it with the magnet a few more times, moving the magnet along the nail or paper clip in only one direction.

> **WORDS TO KNOW**
>
> **attract:** a force that pulls things closer.
>
> **mineral:** a naturally occurring solid found in rocks and in the ground. Rocks are made of minerals. Gold and diamonds are precious minerals.
>
> **lodestone:** a naturally occurring mineral with magnetic properties.
>
> **magnetize:** to make magnetic.
>
> **magnetism:** a force that creates a push or a pull on magnetic objects.
>
> **compass:** a device with a magnetic needle that points north.
>
> **navigation:** planning and following a route.
>
> **Renaissance:** a cultural movement or rebirth that took place in Europe from the fourteenth through the seventeenth centuries.

History of Magnets

Magnetism was not invented by people—it was discovered. The first evidence of people using magnetic force dates back more than 2,000 years. Both in ancient Greece and ancient China, people were aware of magnetic forces that attracted iron and other metals.

In ancient China, people discovered that a magnetic bar of lodestone always pointed in the same direction. They used this discovery to create the earliest form of the **compass**. They didn't understand the science behind magnetism, though, and thought of magnets as mystical objects.

By the 1100s, compasses were used regularly for **navigation** in different parts of the world. However, it wasn't until the **Renaissance** period (between the fourteenth and seventeenth centuries) that people began scientific investigations of magnets and Earth's magnetism.

WACKY CONTRAPTIONS

WORDS TO KNOW

repel: to push away.

electricity: a form of energy caused by the movement of tiny particles called electrons. It provides power for lights, appliances, video games, and many other electric devices.

magnetic field: the area around a magnet in which its magnetic force is felt.

pole: on a magnet, the north or south end where the magnetic field is strongest.

HOW DO MAGNETS WORK?

Let's start with the basics. Magnetism is the force exerted by a magnet as it attracts or **repels** objects, creating a pull or a push. In the case of your latest and greatest work of art on the refrigerator, the force of the magnet holds it, and the artwork, to the refrigerator door. Magnetic forces are also an important part of **electricity** and motors. The push and pull forces of magnets turn electricity into movement! We'll learn more about electricity in Chapter 5.

All magnets have a **magnetic field** around them. You can't see the field, but it's there. Think of it as a magnet's force field—within that field is where its powers work. Once a magnetic object enters a magnetic field, it is attracted to the magnet.

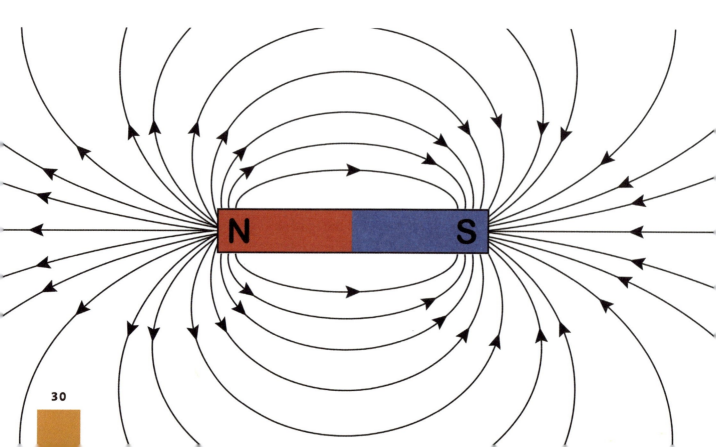

AMAZING MAGNETS

We use magnetic field lines to represent a magnet's magnetic field and the direction the forces move in. These lines around a magnet always form closed loops. The magnet's forces are strongest where the lines are closest together, near a magnet's **poles**. Every magnet has two poles, a north and a south pole.

Have you ever heard the expression "opposites attract"? When you put the north end of one magnet near the south end of another, they attract each other and stick together. On the other hand, if you try to put two north poles or two south poles together, they repel each other.

Magnets get their name from the region of Magnesia in ancient Greece where large pockets of lodestone were first discovered.

Do you have two magnets in your house? (A good place to look is on the refrigerator.) First, set them on the table and move two ends toward each other. Do they attract or repel each other? Next, find objects in your home that are made of metal. Move one of the objects closer and closer to one of the magnets. How far away was it when the magnet attracted it? Once the object entered the magnet's magnetic field, it was attracted to the magnet and pulled toward it. Can you visualize the field around the magnet?

For a review of potential and kinetic energy in contraptions, watch this video about Energy Transfer Machines. How does this contraption show the different transfers of energy?

🔍 Energy Transfer Machines

Magnets even work in water! Try using a magnet to attract a paper clip in a bowl of water. Is the magnetic field the same under water as it is on the table? You can play with magnets more by moving them around beneath a piece of paper, cardboard, or the table with a magnetic object above. It will look as though the magnetic object is moving all on its own.

31

WACKY CONTRAPTIONS

> **WORDS TO KNOW**
>
> **levitate:** to rise and hover in the air.
>
> **maglev:** a transportation system where trains glide above a track using the power of magnets.
>
> **electromagnet:** a magnet that uses electricity to create a magnetic field.
>
> **current:** the flow of electricity.
>
> **technology:** tools, methods, and systems used to solve a problem or do work.

Now, it is time to find out which everyday objects are magnetic and which are not. Find a few objects to test, such as a marble, pair of scissors, popsicle stick, pushpin, and plastic object. What do you think will happen when you move a magnet toward them? Are the objects magnetic or non-magnetic? Keep your discoveries in mind for your next wacky contraption projects.

EARTH IS A MAGNET

If you have ever used a compass, you've used Earth's magnetic field to find your way. That's because our planet is one enormous magnet! As with all magnets, it has a north and a south pole. The movement of molten iron in the outer core of the planet is what generates the magnetic field.

Compasses contain a magnetized needle that has a north and south pole. The needle sits on a point so it can spin freely. As it spins, the needle aligns with the magnetic field of Earth. When people learned about magnets and realized a magnet would point north/south, they defined the north pole of the magnet as the end that points north.

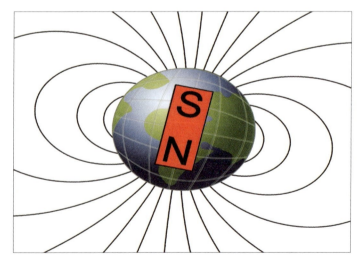

Since opposite poles attract, if the north pole of the magnet is attracted to the geographic North Pole, that must be earth's magnetic south pole! Earth's North and South Poles switch places approximately every 300,000 years because of the constant changes in the forces that create the planet's magnetic field.

AMAZING MAGNETS

To find north, line up the needle with the north markings on the compass. Now you know where each direction extends from where you stand.

Magnets can lose their magnetism when exposed to high heat or an oppositely aligned magnetic field. That's why when you make a magnet, you always need to stroke it in one direction.

Magnets Make Trains Float

Magnets are even used for trains! Some train systems use magnets to make the ride faster and smoother. The use of magnets on the trains and tracks makes the train **levitate** a few millimeters above the rails. These trains are called **maglev**—short for magnetic levitation—trains.

Maglev trains take advantage of the way poles on a magnet repel each other. When the poles of the magnets on both the train and the track repel each other, the train is raised off the track, eliminating friction between track and train.

Not only do the trains utilize super-powerful **electromagnets** to levitate above the track, these magnets also power the trains. The push and pull of alternating **currents** propel the train along the track. Because these magnets are so strong and there's no friction between the train and the track, maglev trains can travel at speeds of more than 300 miles per hour.

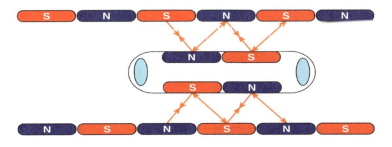

See maglev trains in action in this short video. How does the maglev **technology** deal with friction?

🔍 Interesting Technology MagLev

33

WACKY CONTRAPTIONS

WORDS TO KNOW

migration: the movement of a large group of animals, such as birds, due to changes in the environment.

medical resonance imaging (MRI): a medical test that produces detailed images of the inside of the human body.

organ: a part of the body with a special function, such as the heart, lungs, brain, and skin.

gauss: the measurement of a magnet's strength.

aqueduct: a network of channels used to move water across long distances.

MAGNETS, MAGNETS EVERYWHERE!

Magnets are at work all around us. In addition to being used to display artwork and latch cabinet doors, they fasten some bags and wallets. Many screwdrivers are magnetized, which keeps a screw from falling to the ground before you can fasten it to a surface. A few of your toys likely use magnets, too (go look!).

Many animals, such as bees, birds, and fish, use Earth's magnetic field during their seasonal migrations.

Magnets are used to create electricity and move things, and they are used to store data in things such as computers, flash drives, and credit cards. Televisions, cars, and speakers also use magnets. Even earbuds have tiny magnets. Magnets are at work in doorbells, alarm systems, and roller coasters.

For a deeper dive into Earth's magnetic field, visit this Kiddle website. How might the changes in Earth's magnetic field affect migrating animals?

🔍 Kiddle magnetic field

Doctors use magnets, too. They use **magnetic resonance imaging (MRI)** to see what is going on inside a person's body. The MRI's magnetic field is used to generate a picture of a patient's **organs**.

How can you use magnets in your contraptions? Think about the ways you can employ magnets to create a push or a pull. You might try using a magnet to remove a wedge holding something such as a ball in place or to pull something down. Experiment!

AMAZING MAGNETS

SIMPLE MACHINE #2: THE INCLINED PLANE

Another simple machine that is essential to contraption-building is the inclined plane. An inclined plane is simply a flat surface with one end raised higher than the other—a ramp! Inclined planes are used to move objects up more easily by spreading the work out over a longer distance. You perform the same amount of work, but you need less force. The steeper the inclined plane, the more force you need to move an object. Inclined planes are also used to move things down—the steeper the plane, the faster the object moves.

The strength of a magnet is measured in gauss. The Earth's magnetic field measures between 0.25 and 0.65 gauss. And believe it or not, your fridge magnets are much stronger, with a measurement of 100 gauss.

Where can you find inclined planes in the real world? Check out the front of public buildings and you'll likely see a ramp for people to use to get to the entrance. People have been building and using ramps since ancient times. Egyptians used dirt ramps to build pyramids. People in ancient Rome built giant ramps called **aqueducts** to supply water to the city. Some of those aqueducts are still in use today!

WACKY CONTRAPTIONS

In a contraption, inclined planes can help you control the speed of an object moving down a ramp. The inclined plane allows you to increase or decrease the amount of force the moving object applies to other objects at the end of the ramp. In addition, you can use inclined planes to move objects over long distances and to change the direction of their movement.

> **Still have questions about magnets?** Try this video that breaks down some confusing ideas! Why do farmers feed magnets to their cows?
>
> 🔎 SciShow magnets

Buy It!

Advertisers build contraptions, too! Since contraptions capture people's attention and are fun to watch, several companies including Honda, Samsung, and Target have advertisements that feature a chain reaction.

Honda's ad, "The Cog," uses various car parts to transfer energy throughout the contraption to tip a ramp that allows a new car to roll off. In the Samsung "Smart Travel Rube Goldberg Machine" ad, many different Samsung products are part of the chain reaction that finishes packing a suitcase. Target's "Fresh Machine" ad incorporates a variety of fresh fruits and vegetables as well as different kitchen items to put a slice of tomato on a burger.

What simple machines can you spot in these contraptions? What kinds of products do you use that would benefit from a wacky contraption commercial?

🔎 Samsung Rube Goldberg   🔎 Target Fresh Machine   🔎 Honda The Cog   🔎 Rube Goldberg Sizzle Reel 2022

36

AMAZING MAGNETS

You can use any flat object with one end raised as an inclined plane. That includes books, CD cases, pieces of cardboard or wood, pizza and cereal boxes, notebooks, etc.

Why not scavenge through your old toys for car and train tracks? Empty toilet paper, paper towel, and wrapping paper tubes also make great inclined planes.

The famous Trevi Fountain in Rome, Italy, is still fed by aqueduct. The Acqua Vergine aqueduct carries water to the fountain from about 6 miles outside the city.

ESSENTIAL QUESTION

How can you use the pushing and pulling forces of a magnet to change the direction and speed of a moving object?

TEXT TO **WORLD**

Why is it important to have ramps on public buildings?

37

RING A BELL

Start simple with this first magnet challenge: use a magnet to create a pull to move an object. Easy, right?

> **Challenge Identified.** Set up a contraption that will ring a bell and use an inclined plane and a magnet's pull.

> **If you want to add something unusual to your contraption, make magnetic slime!** Check out this website for instructions. How can you use magnetic slime in ways that are different from a traditional magnet?
>
> 🔍 TedEd magnetic slime

> **Brainstorm ideas and supplies.** Clearly, you need a magnet. Ideally, your fridge has a few you can borrow. Your teacher might have magnets, too. Of course, you also need a magnetic object for the magnet to attract. Next, what can you use for an inclined plane and what can you use for a bell? If you don't have a bell, what could you use to make a bell or something that rings like a bell? A marshmallow?

> **Draw a plan.** Design this goal-scoring contraption, keeping in mind how to create pull from the magnet, what the pull must move, how the forces should transfer energy from one part of the contraption to another, and how all that fits together. One way to include a magnet's pull is to use one magnet to pull another magnet that's holding something (such as a ball) in place at the top of a ramp.

Atlanta's Magnet Man

In Atlanta, Georgia, Alex Benigno has found an innovative way to use magnets. Fed up with getting flat tires on his bicycle because of nails, screws, and other metals in the streets, he designed and built a device to clean up his route to work. The key component—magnets.

Using a trailer to pull behind his bike and magnets attached to the underside of the trailer, Benigno tried several different designs. Once he was up and pedaling, he collected more debris than he ever imagined. In just eight weeks, Benigno had collected more than 400 pounds of screws, nails, and other metals from the streets.

Now he cycles routes all over the city to pick up as much debris as he can when he has time. Benigno even created a social media account. Not only do local people thank and praise him, but people from around the country beg him to come to their towns. He hopes that others will be inspired to join his effort.

❯ **Build.** Following your plan, set up the bell, the object that will ring the bell, and the inclined plane. Put the magnet and magnetic object in place so that when the object is within the magnet's magnetic field, the magnet attracts the object.

❯ **Test.** Start the chain reaction to ring that bell!

❯ **Evaluate.** Did the bell ring? Could the ring have been louder? Did the magnet create the pull you needed to start and keep the chain reaction going? What could you do differently?

❯ **Redesign.** If the pull from the magnet wasn't strong enough, what can you do to improve it? Could you add more inclined planes and steps to the contraption? Or brainstorm other ways you could ring the bell. Consider using a different type of bell or more than one bell.

GOOOOOAL!

As you have learned, magnets can create both a pull and a push. This time you will use a magnet's push in your contraption.

> **Challenge Identified.** Score a goal with a contraption that uses a magnet's push as well as at least one inclined plane.

> **Brainstorm ideas and supplies.** You will need at least one magnet. You can create a push with a magnet in many ways. If you have two magnets, experiment with the way they repel each other. How could you use that in your contraption?

* One way is to use three steel balls and one strong magnet. Create a track for the steel balls—one option is to glue two straws together side by side, but you might have an even better idea! Place the magnet on the track about an inch from the left end. Place two of the steel balls on the track to the right of the magnet. Then, place the third steel ball to the left of the magnet. Move it forward until the magnet attracts it. What happens?

* Also think about what you could use as an inclined plane, what could serve as a goal, and what kind of object you could score with.

> **Draw a plan.** The contraption in this drawing uses an inclined plane, three steel balls, a magnet, and a track made of straws. How could you add to this? How might you design the contraption differently? What other goals could you create? How could you make this more complicated? Be creative—your aim is to score a goal, but you can make this simple or complicated!

> **Build.** Arrange all the parts of the contraption according to your design, with your magnet poised to create a push and the goal lined up for a score.

To get ideas about how to use magnets in your wacky contraptions, check out these videos. How do the creators use the push and pull of magnets to keep momentum going?

🔍 chain reaction with magnets

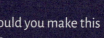

> **Test.** Game on! Set your contraption in motion and watch the points add up.

> **Evaluate.** Did the magnet create the push you expected? Did it create the push in the direction you wanted?

> **Redesign.** How much redesigning does this contraption need? How could you make this contraption more effective? How about more complicated and ridiculous?

CONTRAPTION TIP!
If you cannot find all the supplies you want around the house, try going to a thrift store. Many towns even have stores that carry recycled art supplies.

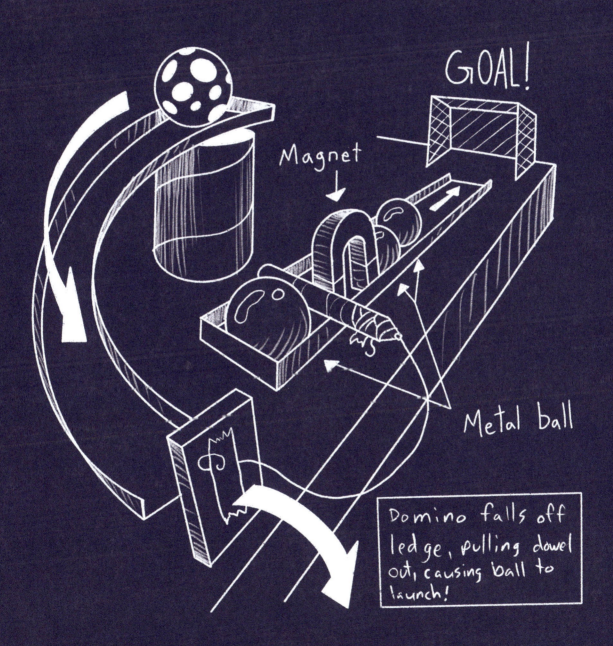

Domino falls off ledge, pulling dowel out, causing ball to launch!

PAPER AIRPLANE LAUNCHER

Now, let's put everything you have learned together! For this challenge, use what you know about magnets as well as elastic potential energy. Remember that you can always use elements from previous contraptions in new contraptions.

> **Challenge Identified.** Create a contraption that uses elastic potential energy and magnets to launch a paper airplane. Bonus points for using a lever and an inclined plane, too.

> **Brainstorm ideas and supplies.** Start with the obvious—you need paper for an airplane, a rubber band, and a magnet. What can you use as a lever and inclined plane? For the airplane, you need a paper clip to attach to the nose of the airplane and then hook onto the rubber band that will launch it. What can you use to build the launch platform? Ideas include cardboard, Legos, and wood. You also need to hold the plane in place on the launcher to maintain the rubber band's potential energy.

> **Draw a plan.** Sketch out the launch platform and the steps leading up to it. How many steps will your contraption have? Where will each part of the contraption be?

> **Build.** Create your launch platform and fold your paper airplane. Then, set up the different parts of your contraption.

> **Test.** Countdown . . . 10, 9, 8, 7, 6, 5, 4, 3, 2, 1!

> **Evaluate.** Did the plane get launched on the first try? This contraption has many different pieces and steps that you need to evaluate. How well did all the pieces work together?

> **Redesign.** Because of the nature of this challenge, you may need to redesign or adjust many parts. Do you need to improve the launch pad and the airplane? Do you need to move things around to improve the chain reaction? If you get things working, consider creating a contraption that launches different types of planes or several planes at once!

If you need ideas about how to make a paper airplane, check out this website. It has many different plane models to choose from, as well as tips and tricks. Which airplane do you think will work best with your launcher?

🔍 Fold'NFly

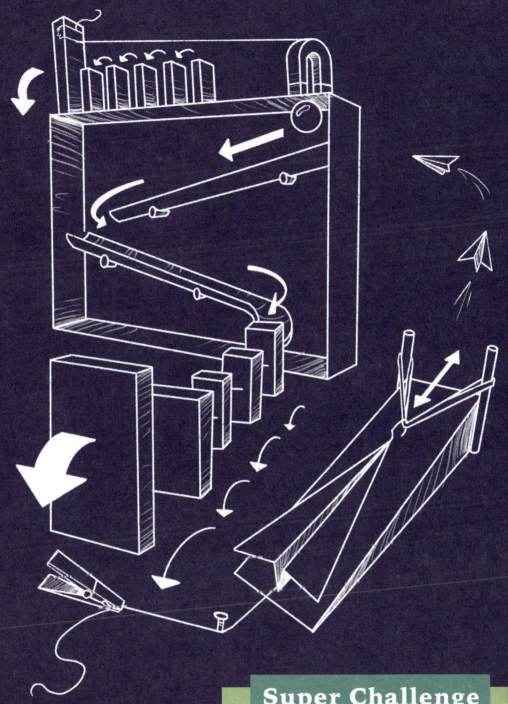

Super Challenge

Make your contraption **nonlinear**—have the chain reaction change direction at least three times. Then, go for five!

WORDS TO KNOW

nonlinear: not in a straight line.

43

Chapter 3

GET GOING WITH
GEARS

Take a look at the wheels on a bicycle. If you don't have a bicycle, look up a picture of one in a book or online. What do you see? **Gears**! Basically, a gear is a wheel and axle with teeth. The wheel is one of the six simple machines that we use to make work easier. A wheel and axle consist of a wheel with a rod of a smaller **diameter** attached to its center. Both the wheel and axle turn together when force is applied to one or the other.

The teeth on a gear are called **cogs**. The cogs are important because they prevent the gears from slipping and keep the gears **synchronized** with each other. Two or more gears together are called a **gear train**. In a gear train, the cogs on each gear fit together, as opposed to on a bicycle, where a chain connects the gears. Gears are used to change the speed, amount, and direction of an **applied force**.

ESSENTIAL QUESTION

How do gears increase the speed or change the direction of an input force?

GET GOING WITH GEARS

THE PHYSICS OF GEARS

Take another look at the bicycle. You'll see that a chain fits around the rim of the gear. Each link of the chain fits over a cog. When you use your feet to pedal, you are applying force to the pedals, making the larger gear turn. The gear moves the chain, which turns the other, smaller gear. Both gears turn in the same direction.

> **WORDS TO KNOW**
>
> **gear:** a wheel with teeth around the rim, used in objects to create a mechanical advantage.
>
> **diameter:** the distance across a circle through its middle.
>
> **cog:** the tooth on the rim of a wheel or gear.
>
> **synchronized:** working together at the same time or rate.
>
> **gear train:** a system of two or more interlocked gears that transmits motion from one gear to the next.
>
> **applied force:** a force that is applied to an object by a person or another object.
>
> **interlock:** to firmly join together, with one part fitting into another.

In a gear train, engineers use two or more **interlocked** gears. In this case, the cogs of one gear fit between the cogs of another gear. As a result of the interlocking cogs, when force is applied to one gear or the other, both move at the same time but in opposite directions. Used this way, gears change the direction of the applied force. If a third gear is added, the two on the ends turn in the same direction, and the one in the middle turns in the opposite direction. What do you think will happen if you add a fourth gear to the train?

> **Watch this video to see how gears and gear trains work.** If you have a gear train with a gear that has 40 teeth and a gear that has 20 teeth, how is the movement of the smaller gear affected when you turn the larger gear?
>
> 🔍 ScienceOnline gear basics

45

WACKY CONTRAPTIONS

WORDS TO KNOW

output force: the amount of force exerted on an object by a simple machine.

terrain: land or ground and all of its physical features, such as hills, rocks, and water.

collision: an event that occurs when a moving object bumps or crashes into another object.

vibrate: to move back and forth or side to side very quickly.

Whenever a larger gear turns a smaller gear, the speed of the smaller gear increases. That's what happens when you ride a bicycle. As you put force on the pedals, the larger gear turns. The chain connecting the two gears then turns the smaller gears and your speed increases.

What happens when a smaller gear turns to move a larger gear? That's when the applied force gets multiplied. Here, the **output force** is greater than the input force. More work is done with less effort.

Many sketches by Leonardo da Vinci (1452–1519)— the fifteenth-century Italian artist, inventor, and engineer— included gears.

The Physics of a Bicycle

Some bikes have only one set of gears—one gear that turns when a force (your feet!) is applied to the pedals. This gear is connected by a chain to a rear gear that turns the bicycle's rear wheel. Other bikes have many gears that you can use to improve your ride.

In bicycles with many gears, you use a lever on the handlebar to change the combination of gears. This is called shifting gears. You shift gears to help you pedal uphill, navigate rough **terrain**, and maintain speed. Shifting from easier to harder gears moves the chain to the biggest front gear and the smallest rear gear so you can pedal faster. The larger gear turns a smaller gear, which increases speed. This gear setting is best for riding along a flat surface and for sprinting.

Shifting from harder to easier gears moves the chain to a smaller gear up front and the largest in the rear to make pedaling uphill easier.

To learn more about bicycle gears and bicycle terminology, watch this video. How can you use this information when you ride a bike?

🔍 TKSST bike gears

GET GOING WITH GEARS

If you have a bicycle with multiple gears, you can shift to a smaller gear in front when going uphill. This allows you to pedal with less force, making it easier to climb the hill.

Gears make work easier in many ways. In physics lingo, gears—similar to simple machines—provide a mechanical advantage. They make work easier, even though the amount of work accomplished is the same.

> **This Next Generation Science video shows gears in action and how they help us do work.** How do gears help people who are fishing?
>
> 🔎 Next Generation gears

Gears allow us to move heavy loads, change the direction of a force, adjust the speed of movement, and transfer motion between different parts of a machine—including wacky contraptions!

Collisions

After building wacky contraptions, you will never think about **collisions** the same way. After all, many actions in contraptions are collisions. Every time two objects collide, energy is transferred from one to the other. Collisions may cause objects to stop moving, fall, or move in a different direction. You might also have figured out through your contraption building that the faster an object moves, the more energy it transfers. Plus, heavier objects can transfer more energy than lighter objects.

Collisions happen in everyday life—and some of those collisions, such as car accidents, can be sad and stressful. But collisions also include fun things, such as a bat hitting a ball for a home run or a bowling ball hitting the pins for a strike. When drumsticks collide with the top of a drum, the energy from the drumsticks transfers to the drum, causing it to **vibrate** and produce sound. And have you ever ridden bumper cars at an amusement park? All those collisions transfer energy. Look around you—what other everyday collisions can you spot?

WACKY CONTRAPTIONS

> **WORDS TO KNOW**
>
> **hobbing machine:** a special tool that cuts the cogs on gears.
>
> **archaeological:** having to do with archaeology, the study of ancient people through the objects they left behind.
>
> **shaft:** a bar that connects one gear to another and transfers power from one to the other.
>
> **rack and pinion gear:** a gear that consists of a toothed rod (the rack) and a circular gear that runs along the rod (the pinion gear).
>
> **rotational force:** a force that causes an object to rotate around a fixed axis.
>
> **linear force:** a force applied along a straight line.
>
> **analog watch:** a watch that shows the time using numbers around the edge and hands that point to the numbers.

THE HISTORY OF GEARS

Gear technology dates back 5,000 years to ancient China, where two-wheeled chariots used gears to help people travel in a consistent direction.

In the fourth century BCE, gears were used in ancient Greece. Greek scientist and philosopher Aristotle (384–322 BCE) noted some of the basic physics of gears and their ability to reverse the direction of applied force.

Archaeological evidence reveals gears being used in waterwheels and clocks.

*Machines that cut gears are called **hobbing machines**. The name comes from a specialized cutting tool called a hob that cuts precise gear teeth for different types of gears.*

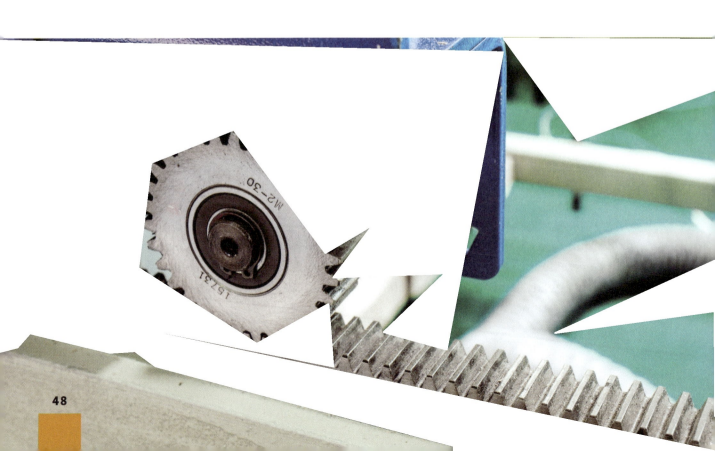

GET GOING WITH GEARS

It wasn't until the 1800s, though, that scientists invented the first machines to cut gears. After that, gears were more widely used. Throughout the 1900s, the technology for cutting gears improved. As a result, machines increasingly included gears. Manufacturers took advantage of gear trains to make machines more efficient. As the automobile industry grew, gears were used in cars, trucks, and other types of vehicles.

Gears are made from many different materials, including steel, plastic, and wood.

Today, we have many different types of gears, each with different functions and used in different industries. For example, a worm gear includes a screw-like **shaft** called a worm and a gear called a worm wheel. Worm gears are used in low-speed conveyor belts and some farm equipment.

The **rack and pinion gear** train looks very different from other types of gears. It consists of a straight rod, called a rack, and a pinion gear that runs along the rack. In this way, a **rotational force** is converted to a **linear force**. This system is used in steering vehicles, lifting things, and more.

Not all gears are round. Watch this video to see square, oval, and other non-circular gears. How do you think these types of gears might be useful?

🔎 TKSST gear shapes

GEARS EVERYWHERE

Once you start looking, you will find gears at work all around you. Does your home have a manual can opener? If so, take a look at it. When you clamp the opener on a can and turn the handle, the interlocking gears turn the blade that cuts through the metal of the can.

Analog watches also have gears. Ask an adult for permission to take the back off a watch so you can see how the gears work together. Many toys have gears, too, including building sets and wind-up or pullback cars. You might already have gears somewhere in your home that you can use in your wacky contraptions!

WACKY CONTRAPTIONS

And even though you can't see the gears, many home appliances—electric mixers, blenders, food processors, washing machines—have them. Gears also control speed and force in power tools such as drills, grinders, and saws.

Cars, planes, and bulldozers use gears. Some elevators make use of gears to control the pulley system to raise and lower the cars. And when you see wind turbines spinning, you're witnessing gears at work!

SIMPLE MACHINE #3: WHEEL AND AXLE

Wheels and axles are helpful for moving things. Imagine if we didn't have them—we would have to push, pull, drag, or carry everything! Wheels help because they reduce the friction and gravity that hinder movement. That makes moving things much easier.

Pullback Cars

Pullback cars are fun to add to any contraption. These simple toys take advantage of gears and the elastic potential energy of a spring.

As you pull one of these cars backward along a surface, the rear wheels and axle turn the gears. This winds up the spring, storing elastic potential energy. The farther back you pull, the tighter the spring coils and the more stored potential energy there is.

When you let go of the car, the potential energy is released and becomes kinetic energy. The car zooms across the surface! If you have a pullback car, experiment a little. Pull it back an inch and measure how far it goes. Repeat the experiment several times, each time pulling the car back a little farther. What ideas does this give you for a contraption?

GET GOING WITH GEARS

Wheels and axles are fun to include in contraptions. They can be used to transfer force, change the direction of the momentum, and more. Remember, the wheel and axle are the basis for gears.

The Red Ball Adventure contraption has lots of interesting elements. Can you spot an element that you can use in your next contraption?

🔍 TKSST red ball marble

Look around your house for toys with wheels. You might find cars or trains. If you don't have any, you can make your own car out of recycled materials.

It's time to put gears to work for you. Use your knowledge of gears to transfer energy in your contraptions. With the right gears, you can speed things up or slow them down. You can also use a small input force from one part of a contraption to turn gears and increase the output force.

ESSENTIAL QUESTION

How do gears increase the speed or change the direction of an input force?

TEXT TO WORLD

Look around your kitchen and find some examples of wheels and gears. How are they different from each other?

CLOSE **A BOX**

Closing a box is not a complicated task, but you are going to make it one! When designing this contraption, you will not only use gears but also wheels and axles.

> **Challenge Identified.** Close the lid of a box to trap a toy figure using gears, wheels and axles, and whatever other objects you want to add. Try to make the chain reaction in your contraption include at least five steps.

> **Brainstorm ideas and supplies.** One of the biggest challenges to this challenge is finding gears. Look through your toys—many toy sets include gears and you may be surprised at what you find. Don't have any toys with gears? You can make your own! What can you use to make the gears? Your gears might look like the ones in the picture, or you may come up with a new design. You also need a set of wheels, a box, and a figure to trap. When making the gears, what did you learn about how cogs and spaces between cogs fit together?

> **Draw a plan.** As you sketch your design, consider how to apply force to the gears and the direction of that input force, as well as the direction of the output force. This will help you decide how many gears to include in your gear train. How will the movement of the gears transfer energy and what will the gears transfer energy to?

> **Build.** Start by positioning the gear train and determining the direction of motion. After that, set up the box and toy figure, the wheels and axles, and the other objects you have decided to include.

> **Test.** Watch out toy figure—the energy in the contraption is headed your way!

> **Evaluate.** Is the poor little toy trapped in the box? If so, well done! If not, what happened? How could it get away?

> **Redesign.** Based on your evaluation, what parts of the contraption need work? Once you fix any problems, could you add other steps to make the contraption even more ridiculously complicated?

Watch this Baker STEM Lab video to see how a group of students used an element they call "tracks and triggers." How can you incorporate this element into your contraptions?

🔍 Baker STEM Rube

Jack-in-the-Box

Jack-in-the-boxes are enduring toys that consist of a box with a lid on a hinge and a crank. When the crank is turned, it plays music inside the box. Eventually, the lid springs open and a "jack" pops up, usually some form of clown or jester.

The toy has a long history, yet no one knows its exact origins. One of the first known jack-in-the-boxes was crafted by a clock maker in Germany during the early 1500s. It was made for a local prince who wanted to give it as a birthday gift for his son. In time, technology allowed for mass production and the jack-in-the-box became a common and popular toy.

Most of the jack-in-the-boxes made today have cute, colorful, fun jacks that pop up. However, some of the older jacks were devilish or even scary.

MOVE A GIRAFFE

Gears come in many different varieties and can be put together to create different gear trains. For this challenge, use gears in a different way from when you were closing a box.

> **Challenge Identified.** Create a contraption that uses gears and wheels and axles, and includes at least five steps, to move a giraffe or other toy animal.

> **Brainstorm ideas and supplies.** Start by considering what this contraption needs to include—gears and wheels and axles. Will you use the gears from the last challenge and put them together in a different way? Make your own? Next, you need a giraffe, though any object will do. How can you move the giraffe?

> **Draw a plan.** Think about where the gears can be in this contraption and how they can transfer energy from one step to the next to keep the chain reaction going. Sketch this out.

> **Build.** Follow your design to set up the contraption and get that giraffe ready to move.

> **Test.** Set everything in motion. Off goes the giraffe!

> **Evaluate.** Did the gears work as you wanted them to? Did the chain reaction keep going until the giraffe was knocked down or did the chain reaction lose momentum?

> **Redesign.** If something didn't work out, how can you modify the contraption? If the contraption worked as you wanted, maybe you want to trying moving the giraffe farther away or use your contraption to move a whole zoo!

OPEN A **HAPPY-FACE-IN-THE-BOX**

You have probably noticed that the challenges in this book are getting more and more complicated. This time you will combine everything you've learned so far to make and open a Happy-Face-in-the-Box.

▶ **Challenge Identified.** Combine gears, magnets, and elastic potential energy in a contraption to open a homemade Happy-Face-in-the-Box. Use a lever, inclined plane, and wheels and axles if you can.

▶ **Brainstorm ideas and supplies.** Think about how to make your Happy-Face-in-the-Box. The design needs to include a spring (made from cardboard maybe?), the box and lid, and the happy face. This challenge requires many items and many steps. Think about how you can use items that you found or created for previous challenges in new ways in this challenge.

▶ **Draw a plan.** Start with the Happy-Face-in-the-Box, focusing on how the lid should open to release the energy stored in the spring and allow the happy face to pop out. Then, sketch out the rest, including how you want the gears to work and in which direction they should turn.

▶ **Build.** Put the Happy Face into the box (storing potential energy!). Then, set up the other items: magnet, gears, inclined plane, lever, and wheel and axle.

▶ **Test.** Ready? Get that wacky contraption moving!

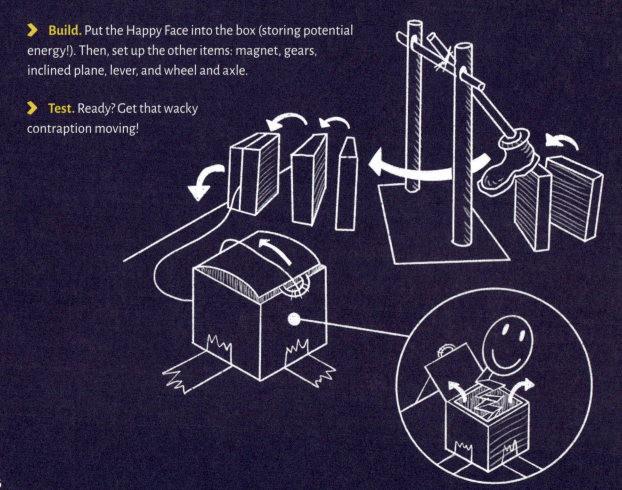

56

> **Evaluate.** Was the Happy Face set free? If not, poor Happy Face. What happened? Did the items work well together or do you need to move things around?

> **Redesign.** After evaluating, do you need to overhaul your contraption completely or maybe just rework parts of it? Remember, testing one step at a time is a good way to identify where the problem might be. Perhaps consider different ways to release the lid from the Happy-Face-in-the-Box and add or move objects around.

Super Challenge

Have all your contraptions been mostly on a flat surface, with energy moving **horizontally**? Time to go vertical! Create a contraption that combines what you've learned while also making the movement in your contraption go up and down.

Music Box Physics

If you wind up a music box (or turn the crank on a jack-in-the-box), music plays. There are no electronic or computer pieces. So, how does it work?

The music is "programmed" on a rotating cylinder called a drum. The drum has small bumps on it called pins. As the drum turns, a metal comb sweeps over it. The comb has teeth of different lengths that each play a different note. When one of the teeth of the comb moves over a pin, it's plucked and plays its note. The placement of the pins on the drum and the unique characteristics of the comb determine the tune that will play.

Music boxes also use tension and gears! When a music box is wound up, a spring coils and tightens (storing potential energy!). Then, when the spring unwinds, it turns a gear. That gear then turns a second gear attached to the drum, making the drum turn and play the tune.

See for yourself how a music box works in this video.
What is the difference in the notes of longer and shorter teeth?

🔍 TKSST music box

WORDS TO KNOW

horizontal: straight across from side to side.

Chapter 4

WHAT'S UP WITH
WATER?

Water is part of our everyday lives. We drink it, bathe in it, and clean with it. Water falls from the sky as **precipitation**. Do you live near an ocean, lake, or river? You might swim, sail, go tubing, or water ski on water.

> **ESSENTIAL QUESTION**
>
> How can water be used to generate energy?

Water takes on a **solid** form when it freezes. Ice cubes keep drinks cool in the summer, and in the winter, lakes and rivers may freeze over. In some places, it snows, sleets, or hails. In other places, water is frozen in the form of **glaciers** or icebergs.

Water can also be a **vapor**—this is water in a **gas** state. Water vapor is an invisible gas. Steam is one type of water vapor, created when water reaches the **boiling point**. And steam contains a lot of stored energy—we'll learn more about steam later in the chapter.

WHAT'S UP WITH WATER?

The Water Cycle

All the water on Earth moves in a continual cycle—precipitation, **evaporation**, and **condensation**. The **water cycle** is the constant movement of water between Earth's surface to the **atmosphere** and back again.

Precipitation is water that falls to Earth as rain, snow, sleet, or hail. As the sun warms water in lakes, rivers, oceans, and other places where water collects, the water evaporates. It turns from its **liquid** form into a gas—vapor—that rises into the air. In the atmosphere, the vapor cools and condenses. It becomes a liquid again and forms clouds. Eventually, it falls to the ground again as precipitation.

WORDS TO KNOW

precipitation: water that falls to the ground in the form of rain, snow, sleet, or hail.

solid: one of the three states of matter. The particles of a solid are bound tightly. A solid has a definite shape and volume and does not flow.

glacier: a slowly moving mass of ice and snow.

vapor: a substance suspended in the air as a gas, such as steam, mist, or fog.

gas: one of the three states of matter. The particles in a gas are not bound to each other and move very fast in all directions. A gas does not have a definite shape or volume.

boiling point: the temperature at which a liquid boils.

evaporation: the process of a liquid heating up and becoming a gas.

condensation: the process of a gas cooling down and changing into a liquid.

water cycle: the continuous movement of water on Earth through the processes of precipitation, evaporation, and condensation.

atmosphere: the blanket of gases surrounding Earth.

liquid: one of the three states of matter. The particles in a liquid cluster together and flow. A liquid takes the shape of its container.

But wait—isn't water vapor invisible? Why can we see steam? The water vapor of steam has already condensed into tiny water droplets in the cooler air. We can see those water droplets. The same is true for clouds, fog, and mist—they are water droplets that have condensed from water vapor in the air.

We use water every day for different things—and it's also a powerful force. Have you ever stood beside a creek when the water is running high? How about beside a waterfall or on a shoreline as waves rush in and out?

WACKY CONTRAPTIONS

WORDS TO KNOW

hydropower: the energy produced by moving water.

turbine: a machine that harnesses the kinetic energy of moving liquids or gases to turn a wheel and generate power.

generator: a machine that converts energy to electricity.

lock: on a river or canal, a system for raising and lowering boats.

Perhaps you've gone rafting down a river or ridden waves on a boogie board in the ocean. You can feel the power of water. Humans have harnessed this energy for thousands of years, and you can use it in your contraptions!

WATER AT WORK

More than 2,000 years ago, the Greeks used the power of moving water from rivers and streams to operate waterwheels. To harness **hydropower**, people directed water moving downstream so it passed over a waterwheel. As the water hit the paddles on the wheel, the force caused the wheel and its axle to turn. In ancient times, grinding stones were attached to the axle, which crushed grain to make flour. As time passed, the waterwheel was adapted for other work, including processing cotton and cutting lumber.

It wasn't until the 1800s, though, that water was used to generate electricity. Wooden waterwheels were replaced with metal **turbines** with propeller-like blades that spin when water flows through them.

Watch this short Next Generation Science video to learn more about how hydroelectric energy is produced. How is the kinetic energy of water harnessed and transferred to businesses and homes?

🔍 Next Gen Sci hydroelectricity

WHAT'S UP WITH WATER?

The spinning turbine is connected to a **generator**, which turns the energy in the moving water into electricity.

We can also use water to help us raise and lower objects, such as boats in **locks**. Humans have been using rivers and canals to transport goods since ancient times. However, in some places, hills and mountains prevented that kind of transport. The invention of locks made it possible to lift boats from lower areas to higher ones.

In a river lock system, a boat traveling upstream enters a lock chamber and the gates close, making the chamber watertight. As more water is added to the chamber, the water level rises, lifting the boat along with it.

Water is essential to life, and more than 70 percent of planet Earth is covered in water. Approximately 96.5 percent of that water is in the oceans.

Cargo ships using a lock on the Panama Canal

WACKY CONTRAPTIONS

WORDS TO KNOW

steam engine: an engine that burns wood or coal to heat water and create steam. The steam generates power to run the engine.

renewable energy: power that comes from sources that will not run out, such as water, wind, and sun.

sustainable: being used without being completely used up or destroyed.

ecosystem: a community of living and nonliving things and their environment.

hydrology: the study of water and how it moves in relation to the land.

drought: a long period of unusually low rainfall that can harm plants, animals, and humans.

Industrial Revolution: a period during the eighteenth and nineteenth centuries when large-scale production of goods began and large cities and factories began to replace small towns and farming.

Think of a rubber duck sitting on the bottom of an empty tub. When the tub is plugged and the faucet turned on, the duck rises with the water. The same thing happens with boats in locks. Once the boat reaches the higher level of the canal, the gates are opened and the boat motors out into the canal. Boats can be lowered by reversing the process.

STEAM POWER

Steam—it's hot and it contains energy. Two thousand years ago, the ancient Greeks figured out that steam can generate movement. Much later, around the year 1700, people began to take advantage of steam power to run machines.

The first crude **steam engines** were used to pump water out of coal mines to help keep the mines from flooding. Throughout the 1700s, inventors worked to improve the efficiency of these steam engines. During the 1800s, steam engines were used to power locomotives and ships, and by the end of that century, steam was the main source of power in transportation.

Hydropower

Hydropower is an important, **renewable energy** source today. In the United States, nearly 7 percent of electricity is generated by hydropower. Of all the renewable energy sources in the United States, hydropower generates around 30 percent by harnessing the power of falling water.

The benefit of hydropower is that it is clean and **sustainable**. For most hydropower sources, dams are built to collect water in reservoirs. In the reservoir, the water has potential energy. Then, water passes downhill through pipes in the dam in the form of kinetic energy. The water spins turbines. The turbines run generators to create electricity.

Although it is a clean and sustainable energy source, hydropower does affect **ecosystems**. Dams block natural migration of fish and change the **hydrology** in an area. Also, during **droughts**, water levels might get too low to generate electricity.

The power of steam is still used today. Most power plants use some type of fuel to boil water, produce steam, and spin turbines to generate electricity. Many places use steam to warm buildings. Have you ever visited a coffee shop? Baristas use steam to make lattes and other drinks. At home, steam power is used in pressure cookers or to cook veggies on the stove.

Steam power was a huge part of the Industrial Revolution between 1760 and 1840, when manufacturing boomed because of developing technology and greatly changed the way people worked.

WACKY CONTRAPTIONS

SIMPLE MACHINE #4: PULLEY

Another simple machine that helps us do work—and create contraptions—is the pulley. A pulley consists of a wheel (often with a groove on the rim) in combination with a cord, rope, or chain. Pulleys are very useful when raising, lowering, and moving objects. Flag poles, elevators, and zip lines all use a pulley system.

Waves in the ocean are another source of energy that can generate electricity!

How could you use a pulley in one of your contraptions? You might find use for a zip line or use a pulley to change the vertical direction of the force in a chain reaction. Some pulley arrangements can be used to increase the mechanical advantage, meaning it requires less force to lift an object.

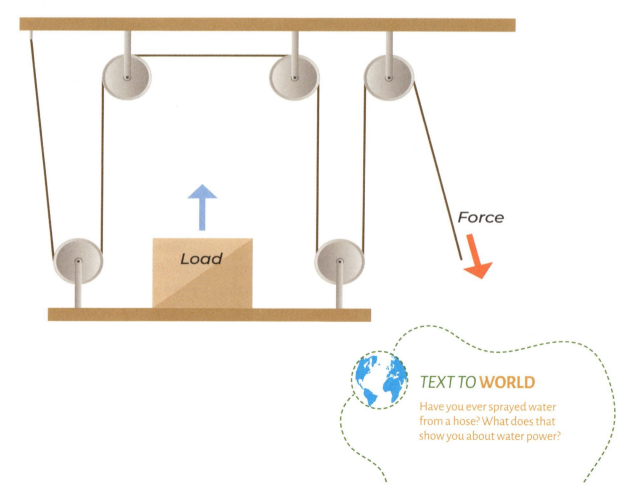

TEXT TO WORLD

Have you ever sprayed water from a hose? What does that show you about water power?

WHAT'S UP WITH WATER?

Inventor of the Dishwasher

If you have a dishwasher in your house, you can thank Josephine Cochrane (1839–1913). During the late 1800s, after several of her valuable dishes were chipped by hand washing, she came up with the idea for a mechanical dishwasher. Her idea included not only racks to hold the dishes in place but also the use of the power of water to rinse and clean them.

Cochrane received a patent for her dishwasher in 1886 and turned her idea into a reality. At the time, traveling and selling her invention took an act of courage—society wasn't accepting of female businesspeople—yet she sold her invention to hotels. In 1893, Cochrane's mechanical dishwasher was on exhibit at the World's Columbian Exposition in Chicago, resulting in a lot of publicity. Since then, technology, including heated water, has improved dishwasher functions. Modern dishwashers use less water than hand washing, and their cleaning products are more effective, which means less strain on the environment. Today, dishwashers are standard in most homes in the United States.

You do not need actual pulleys to use them in a contraption. You can use objects such as empty thread or wire spools, push pins, and Lincoln logs to make pulleys. You can also loop a string or rope over a bar or through a hook to create a pulley-like element in your contraption.

Let's get building! How can you use the power of water in your contraptions? Could you harness the power of falling water to turn waterwheels, use water to lift or lower an object, or apply pressure from jets of water to move objects? Lots of options! If you want to use steam power, ask an adult for help.

ESSENTIAL QUESTION

How can water be used to generate energy?

POUR A BOWL OF CEREAL

Getting a bowl of cereal in the morning is a simple task. But why not use the force of water to turn a waterwheel to power a contraption that pours the cereal for you?

> **Challenge Identified.** Create a contraption that uses a waterwheel and another simple machine, the pulley, to pour a bowl of cereal.

> **Brainstorm ideas and supplies.** The place to start might be the waterwheel. What can you use to make it? Cut up plastic that you found (and washed)? Cardboard?

* Decide how you can incorporate a pulley. Pulley systems do not need to be complex. A piece of string looped through a hook or over a bar at a higher level will work as a fixed pulley.

* Don't forget you need a cereal box and a bowl, as well as a water source to power the waterwheel!

> **Draw a plan.** What should the waterwheel do when it turns? How can you tip the cereal box to pour cereal into the bowl?

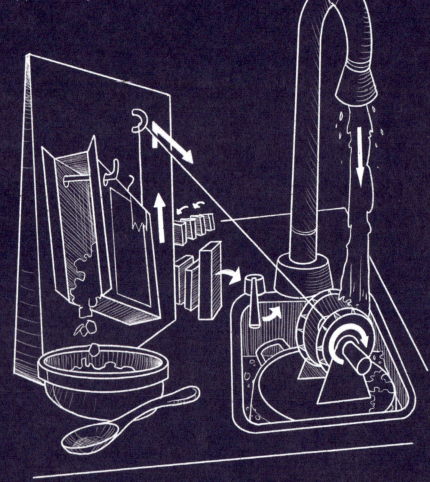

> **Build.** Position all the pieces of the contraption according to your drawing and get ready to eat!

> **Test.** Wait! Before you start the chain reaction, think about the water and where it will go. Do you need to have towels handy? Move to a bathtub? Kitchen sink?

> **Evaluate.** Are you eating a bowl of cereal right now? Did the waterwheel work as you wanted? Was there too much force from the water source or too little? Consider how you can adjust the force so you get exactly what you need. Did the pulley work? Also, look at how much of the cereal actually landed in your bowl!

> **Redesign.** Adjust your contraption as needed to increase or decrease force. Maybe you want to take your contraption to the next level, not only improving on parts that didn't work as expected, but also adding a step that pours milk into the bowl.

It's likely you don't have a waterwheel sitting around your home. But you can make one! You can find plenty of resources online. After looking at a couple different options, do you see any similarities between them?

🔎 Little Bins Big Hands water
🔎 Nanogirl waterwheel
🔎 Education.com waterwheel

Stage Rigging

If you've ever been in a play on a stage or seen a live performance, pulleys were likely an important piece of behind-the-scenes stage equipment. The use of pulleys begins at the start of act one, when the curtains are opened. Large, heavy curtains are opened using a pulley system that converts a linear downward force into a horizontal one.

Pulleys are used throughout many productions. Using pulleys, rigging systems can raise, lower, and move many theater components. They are used to move lights or props. Sometimes, they are even used to raise a performer! The system uses both pulleys and weights to balance a load. Depending on the venue, the rigging systems may be very simple and perform basic tasks. Other rigging systems are quite complicated. However they're used, the pulleys make the behind-the-scenes work much easier!

BOWL A STRIKE

Time to set up a bowling alley right in your house!

> **Challenge Identified.** Design and build a contraption of five or more steps that uses water and a pulley to bowl a strike.

> **Brainstorm ideas and supplies.** What can you use for a bowling ball and pins? You could go big and use cereal boxes as pins and a utility ball to bowl with, or you could go smaller and use dominoes and a marble. Since this challenge involves water, how can you use the power of water to maintain the momentum in the chain reaction? Can you use water in a different way than you did in the first challenge? What can you use for a pulley system?

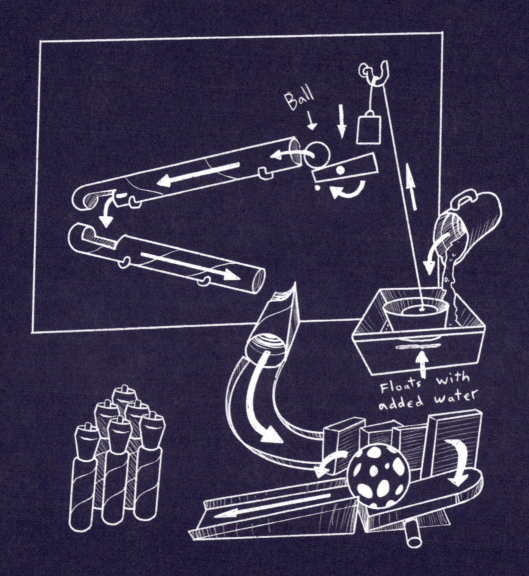

> **Draw a plan.** Create a drawing of your contraption that includes all the objects and steps you want to include in the chain reaction. As you design, think through how you can use water and what kind of mess it might make!

> **Build.** Consider doing this in the bathroom or outside. Assemble your contraption, ready the bowling ball, and set up the pins.

> **Test.** It's the first frame of the game and it's your turn—bowl!

> **Evaluate.** Was it a strike? A split? A gutter ball? Did the water element work like you expected or does it need fine-tuning? Did you make a big mess?

> **Redesign.** If you didn't bowl a strike, it is time to redesign. Perhaps you need to reimagine the pulley system or determine how to apply more (or less) force with the water or maybe you just need to shift, remove, or add a few things.

CONTRAPTION TIP!

If you have a swirly straw or similar type straw, you can pour water into it, move the water down and around, and create a jet of water when it comes out the other end. You can use the force of the water from the jet to move objects.

Game On!

You are not the only one who has fun with wacky contraptions. Back in the 1960s, the Ideal Toy Company created a game, Mouse Trap, inspired by Rube Goldberg's contraption cartoons. As players move their game pieces (tiny mice), they take turns building a contraption to trap an opponent's mouse. The last un-trapped mouse wins. Nowadays, there are video games that incorporate Rube Goldberg machines. Have you ever played one?

DELIVER A MESSAGE

This will not be stealthy note-passing under a desk or sending a text. But delivering a note via a complex contraption will be much more fun.

> **Challenge Identified.** Create a complex contraption of 5 to 10 steps that delivers a note via zip line. Use the power of water in a new way and incorporate as much of what you have learned as possible: elastic potential energy, gears, magnets, and the four simple machines you've learned about so far (inclined planes, levers, wheels and axles, and pulleys).

> **Brainstorm ideas and supplies.** Got a super soaker? That will create a jet of water. That force can be used to do all kinds of things in a contraption (plus it's fun). A zip line simply requires a rope or string and a pulley. How can you hold the pulley at the top of the zip line? Find, create, or reuse other elements from previous contraptions to meet this challenge. You need a note, too—what will it say and where will you deliver it?

> **Draw a plan.** Sketch out the various steps to make this contraption work. Consider making a checklist of the various pieces you want to include. Where is the water going to come in?

> **Build.** String that zip line, write a note, and put the rest of your note-delivery system together.

> **Test.** Get that message out for delivery!

> **Evaluate.** Note delivered? How did all the elements work together? Did some elements perform better than others?

> **Redesign.** If the note was not delivered, think about the transfer of energy from one part of the contraption to the next. How can you apply the right forces in the right places to keep the chain reaction going? Try again!

Super Challenge

Use the power of water in two or three different ways to create a contraption with at least 10 steps.

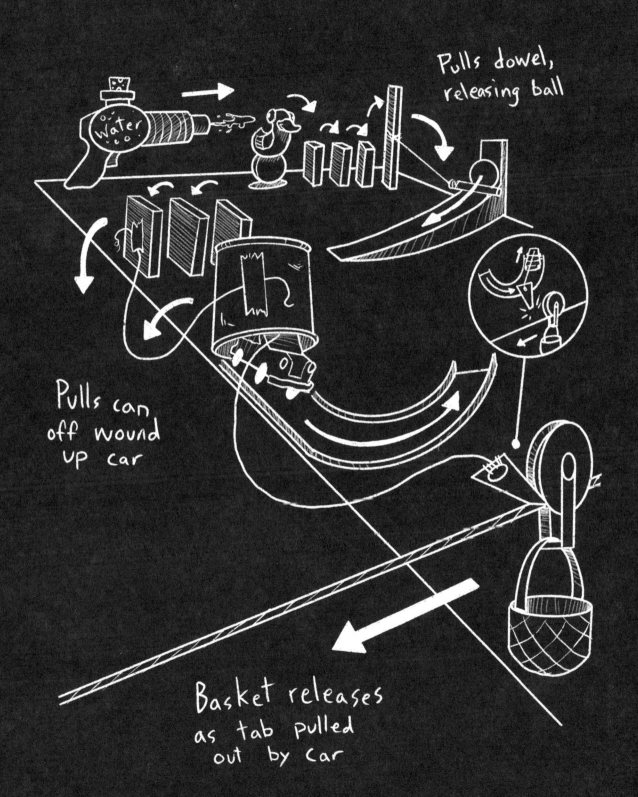

Chapter 5

MAD ABOUT MOTORS, BATTERIES, &
ELECTRICITY

 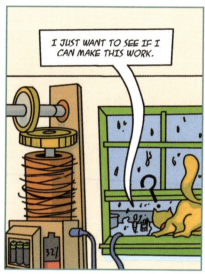 

Most of the time we don't think much about electricity. We flip light switches off and on. We plug in our devices to power and charge them. We pop food in a microwave and throw our clothes in a washing machine. Electricity makes all this possible. But what is electricity?

The simple answer is that it's the stuff that powers our stuff. To explore a fuller answer, you need to know a few things about **atoms**. Atoms are tiny particles that are the building blocks of everything in the **universe**. Planets are made of atoms. **Continents** are made of atoms. Your home is made of atoms. Your pet is made of atoms. This book is made of atoms. Even you are made of atoms!

ESSENTIAL QUESTION

What is electricity and how can we harness it to do work and power wacky contraptions?

MAD ABOUT MOTORS, BATTERIES, & ELECTRICITY

Think of one atom as a Lego brick. Each brick is a building block for whatever you want to create. Atoms are similar, though much, much smaller. In fact, they are so small, their size is measured in **nanometers**. A nanometer is one-billionth of a meter! Millions of atoms would fit on the tip of a pencil.

Atoms are small—and they are made up of even smaller particles. The particles inside an atom are **protons**, **electrons**, and **neutrons**.

Protons and neutrons are found at the center of an atom, in the **nucleus**. Electrons spin very, very, very fast in **orbits** around the nucleus. Electrons can also move between atoms. When they do, they create an **electric current**.

WORDS TO KNOW

atom: a small piece of matter made of protons and neutrons orbited by electrons.

universe: everything that exists everywhere.

continent: one of the earth's large landmasses, including Africa, Antarctica, Australia, North America, South America, and Asia and Europe (called Eurasia).

nanometer: a very small unit of measurement, just one-billionth of a meter.

proton: a positively charged particle located in the nucleus of an atom.

electron: a negatively charged particle that spins in an orbit around the nucleus in an atom.

neutron: a particle in the nucleus of an atom that does not have a charge.

nucleus: the center of an atom, which contains protons and neutrons.

orbit: the path of an object circling another object.

electric current: the flow of electricity.

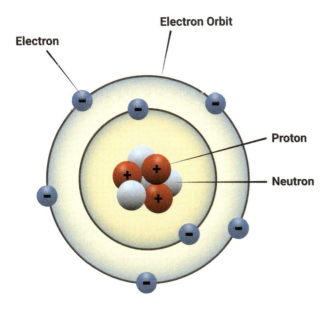

Electricity is a form of kinetic energy.

WACKY CONTRAPTIONS

WORDS TO KNOW

static electricity: an imbalance of electrical charges caused by transferring electrons from one object to another.

electrical charge: a fundamental property of matter. Protons have a positive charge, electrons have a negative charge, and neutrons have no charge.

discharge: the sudden flow of electrons from one object to another.

STATIC ELECTRICITY

Electricity comes in two forms. Have you ever walked across a carpet and then touched a doorknob and been shocked? Did your clothes stick together after coming out of the dryer? That is **static electricity**, created by friction between two surfaces.

Static electricity is simply the buildup of an **electrical charge** on an object. Static electricity doesn't flow like electricity through a current.

Most of the time, the protons and electrons in matter are balanced, or neutral. But electrons like to move around. When you rub two objects together and cause friction, this encourages electrons to move to atoms in other objects. This leaves one object with more protons, so that object becomes positively charged. The object the electrons move to becomes negatively charged.

OK Go!

The music group OK Go built a wacky contraption for a music video for its song, "This Too Shall Pass." The chain reaction machine was built in a warehouse. It features not only dominoes and balls rolling down ramps and other simple machines but also tower twisters, a catapult, water, pendulums, a falling piano, and more. The chain reaction is precisely timed to the song, and one element even plays some of the music! It took several months of planning, designing, and building, plus dozens of people, to create the video. They also had to do more than 60 takes to get it right.

 Watch the OK Go video carefully. Can you spot each of the six simple machines in the contraption? What elements of physics do you see at work?

OK Go "This Too Shall Pass"

MAD ABOUT MOTORS, BATTERIES, & ELECTRICITY

Have you ever slid down a slide and had your hair stand up? This happens because negatively charged electrons are removed from your body due to the friction. Since each hair is left with the same positive charge, they all try to push away from each other and end up standing up straight.

The word *static* means "at rest or not moving."

As with a magnet, if two objects have a buildup of similar charges, they repel each other—that's what happens to your hair on a slide. But if they have a buildup of opposite charges, they attract each other. Some materials pick up electrons easily, while others give them away easily. Have you ever found your socks stuck to each other in the dryer? That happens because of static electricity!

When you touch a doorknob and get a shock after walking across a carpet, you are experiencing a static **discharge**. It's nature's way of finding a balance of protons and electrons. The electrons flow suddenly to where they are needed to create a balance.

Do you have a balloon? Blow it up and tie it off. Now, rub it on your hair or clothing for a few seconds. Does it stick to the wall? If it does, you're seeing static electricity in action! Rubbing the balloon causes a buildup of electrons, which have a negative charge. When you put the balloon against the wall, the built-up electrons are attracted to the protons in the atoms in the wall, which hold the balloon in place.

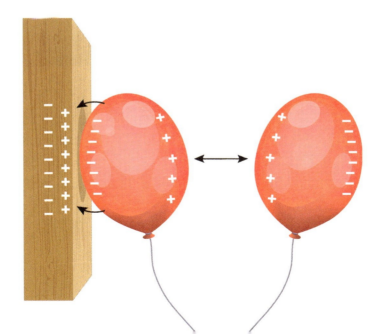

75

WACKY CONTRAPTIONS

> **WORDS TO KNOW**
>
> **circuit:** a complete path of an electrical current.
>
> **conductor:** a material through which electricity can move quickly and easily, which includes most metals.
>
> **insulator:** a material such as plastic or rubber that does not allow electricity to pass through easily or at all.
>
> **volt (V):** the unit used to measure the electric potential between two spots in a circuit.

Aside from sticking balloons to walls, does static electricity have any real uses? Yes! Static electricity is used in photocopiers and printers, where it attracts ink to the paper. Static electricity is also used in air filters, dust removal systems, and paint sprayers.

ELECTRIC CURRENT

Unlike static electricity, an electric current is the flow or movement of an electrical charge through a path, or **circuit**. This is the electricity we use to power our everyday lives. How?

Since protons have a positive charge and electrons have a negative charge, the electrons normally stay close, orbiting the nucleus. When an outside force is applied to the atom, electrons might be knocked loose so they move to another atom. This movement creates an electric current, which is a form of kinetic energy. Stored electric energy, as in a battery, is a form of potential energy—but more on batteries later.

> **This PBS video titled *Static Electricity: Snap, Crackle, Jump* shows static electricity in action.** What experiments can you do with static electricity?
>
> 🔎 PBS snap crackle pop

We know electrons move in all materials. However, they move more easily in some than in others, and these materials are called **conductors**. Wires that carry electricity are made of conductive materials, such as copper. They are usually coated in an **insulator**, such as plastic or rubber, that does not allow electrons to move through them easily and keeps energy from being lost. Insulators also prevent us from being shocked by wires that are conducting electricity.

MAD ABOUT MOTORS, BATTERIES, & ELECTRICITY

To conduct, or move, electricity, we need a complete, closed circuit for the current to follow. As long as the electricity has an energy source such as a battery and an uninterrupted circuit, it keeps flowing. If you interrupt that flow, the electricity stops flowing.

Go turn on a light. When the light turns on, you have completed a circuit and electricity is flowing. Now, turn it off. By flipping the switch, you have broken the circuit and electricity cannot flow to the light. The same is true for a battery-powered flashlight. Turning the switch on completes the circuit and turning it off breaks the circuit.

If you get shocked by static electricity, the shock may be thousands of volts (V)! However, because there is little current and it lasts for only a short time, it is not powerful enough to harm you.

WHERE DOES ELECTRIC CURRENT COME FROM?

Electric current starts with a power source, such as fossil fuels or renewable energy. Fossil fuels include coal, oil, and natural gas. Wind, sun, and water are renewable energy sources.

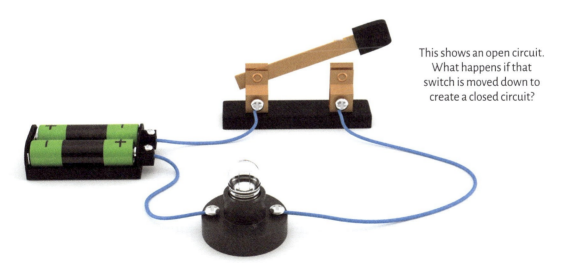

This shows an open circuit. What happens if that switch is moved down to create a closed circuit?

WACKY CONTRAPTIONS

WORDS TO KNOW

voltage: the force of an electric current, measured in volts.

galvanized: coated with a layer of zinc.

electrolyte: in a battery, a gel or liquid that conducts electricity.

chemical energy: energy from a chemical reaction.

chemical reaction: the rearrangement of atoms in a substance to make a new chemical substance.

electrode: a conductor through which electricity enters or leaves an object such as a battery.

Most of the world's electricity is generated in a power station using one of these sources of energy to heat water to create steam that spins a turbine. The turbine powers a generator that converts the kinetic energy of the turbine into electrical energy by spinning coils of wire inside a strong magnet.

Voltage is the push that makes electrical charges move in a wire. One way to think about voltage is that it is similar to water pressure—just as water pressure pushes water through pipes, voltage pushes electricity through wires.

It's almost always possible to trace the origins of any renewable energy source to the sun! The warmth of the sun causes wind. Sunshine is needed for biofuel to grow, and the sun powers the water cycle.

Potato Battery

Did you know that you can make a battery using a potato? It's true! Using copper pennies, a **galvanized** nail, insulated wire, and a potato, you can generate approximately 0.5 volts, sometimes more.

How? Regular batteries create electrical energy as a result of a chemical reaction between two metals and an **electrolyte**. The potato works similarly. In a potato battery, the chemical reaction occurs between the copper of a penny, the zinc of a nail, and the juices inside a potato, which produces electrical energy that allows a current to flow.

For further instructions on building a potato battery, and different ways to build it, visit this site.

🔎 STEM Generation potato

MAD ABOUT MOTORS, BATTERIES, & ELECTRICITY

BATTERIES

Batteries provide another source of power. A battery has chemical potential energy—it converts that **chemical energy** into electrical energy.

Remember—electrons need to come from somewhere and flow somewhere else. In the battery, a **chemical reaction** moves electrons when the battery is part of a closed circuit. They move from the negative **electrode** of the battery to the positive electrode via the circuit. Without a closed circuit that has a good conductor to connect the negative and positive battery electrodes, no chemical reaction takes place and no electrical current flows.

To understand how much batteries are part of our everyday lives, go on this battery scavenger hunt. How many batteries did you find? Is the number what you expected or were you surprised?

🔍 ACM battery hunt

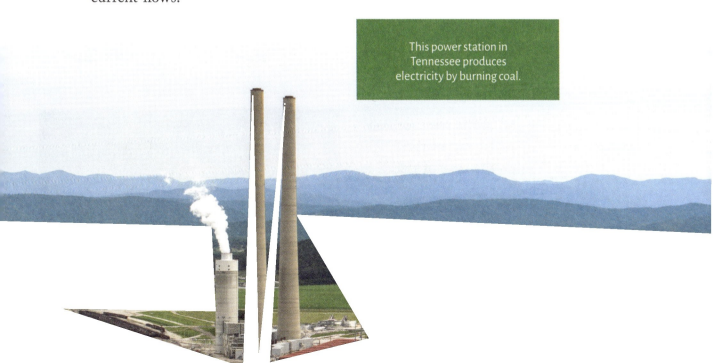

This power station in Tennessee produces electricity by burning coal.

WACKY CONTRAPTIONS

WORDS TO KNOW

oxidation: the loss or transfer of electrons.

corrode: to rust.

axis: an imaginary line around which an object rotates.

thread: the raised edge of a screw that winds around.

adapter: a device for connecting two parts (as of different diameters) of an apparatus.

As in other electrical circuits, battery power is measured in volts. Most of the batteries we use in our devices, such as remote controls and flashlights, are 1.5 volts. In contrast, the transmission lines from power stations are more than 200,000 volts! The power coming into most buildings in the United States is between 110 and 120 volts.

Open Circuit **Closed Circuit**

You can create a simple circuit by connecting a conductive wire to each end of a battery. Let's try a simple experiment. You need a D battery, an insulated wire, and a flashlight bulb. For this simple circuit, the bulb needs to be a small flashlight bulb so the battery can power it. Before starting this, make sure the battery and the bulb are both working.

Tape one end of the wire securely to the negative, flat end of the battery. Position the base of the bulb on the other end—the positive, bumpy end of the battery. Make sure the base of the bulb stays in contact with the battery and touch the free end of the wire to the base of the bulb.

> This TedEd video reveals details about how batteries work and the role of electrons and **oxidation**. What did you learn about why batteries die after a certain amount of use? What are the limitations of rechargeable batteries?
>
> 🔍 TEDEd how batteries work

Does it light? If so, you have made a complete, simple electrical circuit! If not, investigate the reasons why the bulb isn't lit. Perhaps the connections are not secure or the wire is damaged or frayed. Try again!

WARNING!

Using electricity and batteries can be dangerous. Make sure you have an adult's permission to use them in your contraptions, especially if you are using them in a new way. Here are a few things to keep in mind.

- Check that the wires or cables are not damaged or frayed.
- Never use an electrical current near water.
- Use caution around electrical outlets—never put a finger or object, other than a plug, into a socket.
- Ask for help if you are going to use appliances.
- Unplug everything after use.
- Do not plug too many appliances into one electrical socket.
- Do not handle or use batteries that are **corroded** or leaking.

SIMPLE MACHINE #5: THE SCREW

Another simple machine is the screw. Look at a screw closely. What do you notice? A screw is simply an inclined plane wrapped around a central **axis**. The inclined plane creates **threads** as it winds around that axis. Screws help us hold things together or lift or lower an object.

Actual screws are examples of this simple machine. Bolts, jar lids, drills, lightbulbs and sockets, circular staircases, spiral marble runs, and even swirly slides are more examples of screws.

Different countries have different voltages coming into their homes and businesses, which is why travelers bring power adapters.

WACKY CONTRAPTIONS

You can use screws in contraptions in lots of ways. One is a spiral marble run. Funnels are also great—they work like screws because an object that you put in a funnel spirals around before coming out the narrow opening. What about swirly straws? You can also make your own screws using old tubing or by cutting up and taping empty toilet paper rolls together.

Time for contraption design! Use your new knowledge about screws and electricity to take wacky contraption building to a whole new level! You can buy supplies or look around your house for items that use electricity and could be incorporated into a contraption. Cell phones run on batteries—you could use a cell phone to generate a vibration and cause objects to move. Perhaps you have toys, such as a remote-controlled car, that use batteries. Lights, flashlights, and fans are also possibilities. Have an open mind as you look for items that use electricity and could be used in your latest and greatest, complicated contraption!

Archimedes invented a kind of screw that could transport water from a lower pool to a higher pool. We still use Archimedes's screw in engineering projects today!

ESSENTIAL QUESTION

What is electricity and how can we harness it to do work and power wacky contraptions?

TURN ON A **LIGHT**

This challenge gives you a chance to shed light on your wacky contraptions. You will use the energy transferred throughout a contraption to complete an electrical circuit that turns on a light.

> **Challenge Identified.** Create a multi-step contraption that turns on a light. Use a screw in some form as well as other things you've learned about.

> **Brainstorm ideas and supplies.** Think about what light you want to turn on. Look around your home for different types of switches that your contraption can easily incorporate. For the screw, maybe find or make a marble run. If you are making one, what could you use?

> **Draw a plan.** You might end up with a contraption that utilizes a marble run as well as a block to pull down on a light switch to turn on a light. But you might have different ideas!

> **Build.** Assemble your ridiculously complicated, wacky, light-turning-on contraption.

> **Test.** Time to shed light on your latest invention!

> **Evaluate.** If the light is on, great work! If not, where in the contraption did the energy transfer stop?

> **Redesign.** If the light didn't turn on, check the steps in the chain reaction and correct whatever prevented the light from turning on. If the light turned on, perhaps you would like to add new steps to make the contraption even more complicated! What else could you add?

Car releases ball, which swirls around until it hits block

83

APPLY A BANDAGE

Do you really need an electric current to apply a sticky bandage to a cut? Not usually! But this time, you do.

> **Challenge Identified.** Create a wacky contraption that utilizes electricity and a type of screw to apply a Band-Aid in a minimum of five steps.

> **Brainstorm ideas and supplies.** These contraptions are getting trickier, aren't they? By now you are an experienced engineer and know how to apply your creativity to the engineering design process. Start by figuring out what you can include that uses electricity—a remote-control car or drone? Another kind of toy? Get creative! The screw for this contraption is challenging, too. You could use a conventional screw. Funnels and spiraled tracks for marbles or cars are also screws. You can even make a screw! Don't forget the bandage!

Electricity is fast! It moves at the speed of light—186,000 miles per second.

> **Draw a plan.** Keep in mind how you want to use the electricity and where the screw fits in. Sketch out all the steps so your contraption finishes by applying a bandage.

> **Build.** Put everything in place and poise that bandage for application. Who will be the recipient?

> **Test.** Prepare to administer first aid!

> **Evaluate.** Did the wound get covered properly? Was there enough force or too much force to apply the bandage at the end? Was electricity a useful element? Did the screw work the way you wanted it to? Look at each element, identifying what worked as expected and what didn't.

> **Redesign.** If necessary, adjust the contraption slightly to better apply the Band-Aid. Maybe you can incorporate electricity in a different way?

Need a glass of milk? Watch this PBS video to learn how kids like you put together this complicated and ridiculous 34-step contraption to perform such a simple task. How did these kids use electricity in their contraption? (Hint: They use electricity more than once!)

🔎 PBS Learning simple machine milk

Movie Night

The movie *Soup to Nuts* was written by Rube Goldberg and directed by Benjamin Stoloff. In the black-and-white film, shopkeeper Mr. Schmidt goes bankrupt because instead of running his costume shop, he spends his time creating Rube Goldberg machines. As the plot thickens, Ted, who works at the shop, and two friends hatch a plan that goes awry. The result is a fire that one of Schmidt's machines ultimately extinguishes.

While Rube Goldberg did not write himself as the main character, he does make a **cameo** appearance in this **slapstick** comedy. Also, the film was the **debut** for the iconic trio, the Three Stooges, who performed together for several decades up until 1970. They were best known for their comedy, mayhem, and verbal bantering.

WORDS TO KNOW

cameo: a single, very brief appearance, especially by a famous person.

slapstick: comedy stressing ridiculous situations and horseplay.

debut: to introduce.

TEXT TO **WORLD**

How would your life be different if we didn't have electricity?

POP A BALLOON

So far, you have learned about elastic potential energy, magnets, gears, hydropower, and now electricity. You have also learned about five of the six simple machines (lever, inclined plane, wheel and axle, pulley, and screw). How many of these can you incorporate into a contraption

> Always be careful with sharp objects. Never aim at people or other living creatures.

> **Challenge Identified.** Create a contraption of at least 10 steps that pops a balloon using electricity and a screw, and as many other things you've learned about as possible.

This Next Generation Science video about circuits shows how a simple serial circuit works. What happens when more and more lightbulbs are added to a single circuit? Why?

NGS serial circuit

> **Brainstorm ideas and supplies.** Start with the end in mind. You need a balloon and something to pop it with. What could you pop a balloon with? What could you attached it to—a lever? A moving car? Something else? Identify how you can use electricity in this challenge. Try to use something you have not used before. A fan? A vibrating cell phone? What could you use as the screw in this challenge? Look back through what you've already used in the challenges in the book and reuse one. Or maybe you're up for creating something new!

> **Draw a plan.** Sketch out the contraption with the objects you have decided to use. How will they work together to keep the momentum going?

Super Challenge

Create a contraption that incorporates electricity in three different ways and has at least a dozen steps. Can you create a contraption that utilizes static electricity?

> **Build.** Blow up the balloon and connect all the objects to ensure a chain reaction. Be sure to keep the balloon popper away from the balloon for now!

> **Test.** All set? Get the energy moving!

> **Evaluate.** Was there enough force to pop the balloon? Was whatever you tried to pop the balloon with sharp enough? Or maybe you need to blow up the balloon more, which makes it easier to pop. What else worked well? What needs attention?

> **Redesign.** Could you put all the objects in the contraption together another way? Think about adding, removing, or rearranging objects or changing steps. Tinker with the contraption and try again!

CONTRAPTION TIP!
A pointed wood screw can be used as a tool to bore holes in plastic and cardboard.

Chapter 6

COUNTING ON CHEMICAL REACTIONS

What do you think of when you hear the term *chemical reaction*? **Scientists in white lab coats mixing up concoctions? The truth is that chemical reactions occur everywhere, not just in labs.**

A chemical reaction occurs when one or more substances change into new and different substances. In some cases, it's easy to tell when a chemical reaction takes place—you mix together ingredients for a batch of cookies and the goopy batter turns into something delicious you can eat. How about an explosion? That's a chemical reaction, too. Other times, chemical reactions are slower and more subtle—rusting iron and ripening fruit are both slow chemical reactions.

> **ESSENTIAL QUESTION**
>
> How is energy used or released in chemical reactions?

88

COUNTING ON CHEMICAL REACTIONS

Chemical reactions occur when substances change and the atoms within them are rearranged. When a substance has undergone a chemical reaction, it might change temperature or form a solid or **emit** light.

Sometimes, you can tell a chemical reaction has occurred if the substance smells differently than it did before. A change in color can also indicate a chemical reaction. At other times, you can tell a chemical reaction occurs when a gas is produced or a liquid becomes bubbly.

The process of water freezing is not an example of a chemical reaction! This is a physical change. Water changes from liquid to solid, but the chemical makeup of the water stays the same.

> **WORDS TO KNOW**
>
> **emit:** to send or give out something, such as smoke, gas, heat, or light.
>
> **ethylene:** a gas produced by many fruits and vegetables that triggers ripening.
>
> **chlorophyll:** the chemical in a plant's cell that gives a plant its green color.
>
> **cell:** the basic part of a living thing. Cells are so small they can be seen only with a microscope. There are billions of cells in most living things.

Think about fruit ripening on the counter. You can spot many signs of a chemical reaction. Fruit produces a colorless gas called **ethylene**. (Some fruits produce a lot, others almost none.) As the fruit matures, it produces more ethylene, which triggers ripening. In this process, starches in the fruit are converted to sugar, making it sweeter. In addition, the **chlorophyll** that makes some fruit green begins to break down and allows the fruit's real colors to emerge. Finally, **cells** within the fruit are broken down in the ripening process, making the fruit softer.

Have you ever eaten a banana that had turned a little brown? How does it feel and taste different from one that's still a little green? Eventually, the ripening process turns into a rotting process as the fruit continues to chemically change and decay. The chemical reactions during ripening change not only what we can see and smell on the outside, but also what the fruit is made of!

WACKY CONTRAPTIONS

WORDS TO KNOW

volume: the amount of space occupied by something.

expand: to spread out and take up more space.

helium: a gas that's lighter than air.

chemistry: the science of the properties of substances and how they interact, combine, and change.

bond: a force that holds together the atoms or groups of atoms in a molecule.

molecule: a group of atoms bonded together, the simplest structural unit of an element or compound. Molecules can break apart and form new ones, which is a chemical reaction.

reactant: a substance being changed in a chemical reaction.

product: the new substance created when two or more substances are combined.

WHAT'S THE MATTER?

To better understand chemical reactions, you need to know a little bit about matter, because matter is at the heart of chemical reactions. Matter is anything that occupies space and has mass.

The most common states of matter are solid, liquid, and gas. Each has different properties, especially with respect to shape and **volume**. Think back to the water chapter. Water occurs in each of these states—solid, liquid, and gas.

- **Solids** maintain their shape and have a fixed volume, such as this book. You can touch and hold solids.

> **Matter is never created, and it is never destroyed. All matter in our world is part of a continuous cycle.**

- **Liquids** also have a fixed volume, but their shapes change to fit the container they're in. If you pour milk into a wide, shallow bowl, it takes the shape of the bowl. If you pour the milk into a tall, narrow glass, it takes a different shape.

- **Gases,** on the other hand, do not have a fixed shape or volume. They **expand** and fill whatever container they are in. Without a container, gases continue to expand and float away. Consider a helium balloon. When **helium** is inside the balloon, it fills the balloon and takes its shape. If you let the helium out, it expands and floats away and the balloon splutters around.

> **Supermarkets use ethylene to ripen bananas on a schedule.** Watch this experiment to see this in action!
>
> 🔎 BBC Earth supermarkets ripen

COUNTING ON CHEMICAL REACTIONS

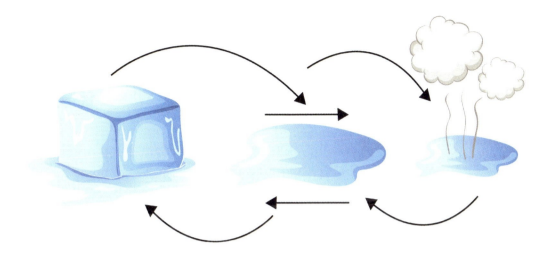

Matter can change from one state to another. It can also change back. The study of matter and how matter changes is the science of **chemistry**!

Think back to the last chapter. What do you think the simplest building blocks of matter are? Atoms! When atoms **bond** together, they form **molecules**. And when molecules combine, they form matter.

The atoms bonded together within molecules are stable. What do you think happens when the molecule breaks up? A chemical reaction takes place! A chemical reaction is just the result of the breakup of atoms.

When the atoms in the **reactant**—or the substance that undergoes the change during a chemical reaction—break their bonds, the atoms move on to find new atoms to bond with and form a new substance. The new substance is called the **product**.

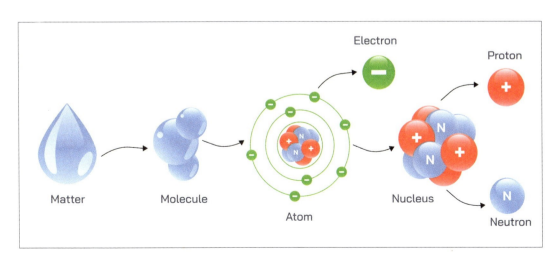

WACKY CONTRAPTIONS

> **WORDS TO KNOW**
>
> **photosynthesis:** the process through which plants use water, carbon dioxide, and sunlight to make their food.
>
> **fermentation:** the chemical breakdown of substances by yeast, mold, or bacteria.

CHEMICAL REACTIONS IN EVERYDAY LIFE

Chemical reactions are going on all around you all the time. In some reactions, energy is used. In other reactions, energy is released.

Do you like baking cookies? When you put cookie dough in the oven, the heat causes a delicious chemical reaction. **Photosynthesis** is another example of a chemical reaction that uses energy.

> **Learn more behind the chemistry of cookies in this TedEd video.** Can you list the series of chemical reactions that occur throughout the process of making cookies?
>
> 🔍 TedEd chemistry cookies

Chemical reactions that release energy usually do so in the form of heat, light, or motion. A burning candle or a campfire releases energy in the form of heat and light. Exploding fireworks also release a lot of energy as heat, light, and noise.

The fuels we use to run our cars and warm our homes have chemical potential energy. Batteries store chemical potential energy, too. Other examples of chemical reactions that release energy are rusting, **fermentation**, bleaching fabric, and souring milk.

Chemical reactions even occur in you! All the food we eat has chemical potential energy, including those cookies. In our bodies, digestion breaks down food and releases that energy to allow us to move, work, play, and grow. The result of the chemical reactions is the fuel that keep us going.

> **When one chemical reaction causes a series of other chemical reactions, can you guess what it's called? A chain reaction!**

Photosynthesis

In plants, chemical reactions take place all the time! Photosynthesis is the way plants make their food. Plants use water gathered from their roots, carbon dioxide from the air, and sunlight. The sunlight provides the energy to start the chemical reaction to combine the water and carbon dioxide. This creates glucose, the sugar plants use for food. It also generates oxygen, which it releases into the air for us to breathe.

You can think of photosynthesis as though plants are cooking their own meal. Plants mix a couple of ingredients (water and carbon dioxide), then use the sun's energy to create a new product!

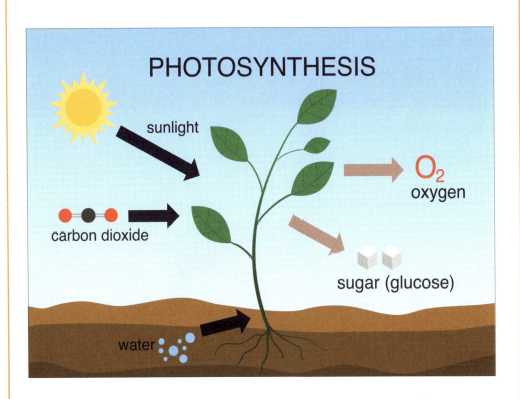

Visit this website to see an infographic and learn more about photosynthesis. What is the role of chlorophyll in photosynthesis?

🔎 Barton photosynthesis

WACKY CONTRAPTIONS

FRIENDLY PUBLIC SERVICE WARNING

Chemistry is fun, but it can be dangerous! Here are a few tips for staying safe while having fun experimenting.

- Always get adult supervision.
- Research your ingredients so that you know what happens when different ingredients are mixed—two ingredients may be harmless alone, but toxic or explosive together.
- Use only ingredients that are properly labeled.
- Keep the ingredients in their original containers unless in use so you know what they are.
- Wear gloves and proper eye protection.
- If possible, do experiments outdoors.
- Never taste or touch the product (unless it's cookies!).
- Dispose of everything properly.

Always wear gloves and safety goggles when working with chemical reactions!

CHEMICAL REACTION EXPERIMENTS

Here are 10 simple and safe chemical reaction experiments. Remember to get adult supervision. Also, have your design notebook handy. Observe what happens when you combine these different ingredients. Identify the chemical reactions taking place.

1 Combine baking soda and vinegar with water and dish soap to make a model volcano!

2 Combine Mentos candy and a 2-liter bottle of soda to create another type of explosion.

> **Chemical reactions have changed the course of history.** Watch this PBS video to learn more. In your opinion, which of these examples had the greatest impact?
>
> 🔍 PBS six reactions

3 Place a raw egg (still in its shell) in a jar with vinegar to see what happens in this slow chemical reaction (this will take one to two days).

4 With an adult's help, pour a tablespoon of nail polish remover (acetone) on a piece of Styrofoam to observe a rapid chemical reaction.

5 Combine white school glue, Borax, and a bit of water to create slime.

6 Open a bottle of clear soda and pour it into a glass. Add raisins and watch them dance.

7 Pour ⅓ cup of oil over ⅔ cup of water in a jar. Add an Alka-Seltzer tablet and watch the fireworks!

8 Grow crystals with a combination of ¼ cup of Epsom salts and a ½ cup of boiling water.

9 Grow your own rock candy with sugar and water (and lots of time)!

10 Send secret messages to your friends with invisible ink! Write with lemon juice on white paper and let it dry. To reveal the message, hold the paper near a warm lamp or other flameless heat source.

After seeing how some simple chemical reactions work, how will you use chemical reactions to keep chain reactions going in your wacky contraptions?

WACKY CONTRAPTIONS

SIMPLE MACHINE #6: THE WEDGE

The sixth and last simple machine is the wedge. Most wedges look like two inclined planes back-to-back, so they are wide at one end and tapered to a sharp point at the other. Wedges split objects apart, separate objects, or hold objects in place. Examples of wedges in everyday life include knives, chisels, axes, and your teeth! Nails and thumbtacks are also wedges. Doorstops are wedges, too.

How might you use as a wedge in a contraption? You could use a wedge to hold something in place until a force removes the wedge. Or you could apply force to a wedge to separate something.

Rockets are blasted into space by a chemical reaction that results from combining liquid oxygen and liquid hydrogen.

Possible materials to use as wedges: nails, pushpins, or scissors (two wedges working together!) or make one out of cardboard.

Now, are you ready for your last set of challenges? Your contraptions have included elastic potential energy, magnets, gears, water, electricity, and chemical reactions. By the end of this chapter, you will have incorporated all six simple machines. Rube Goldberg would be impressed!

Through hands-on trial and error, you have also learned a lot about physics and how forces interact with each other. Without knowing it, you have become a master machine maker. Your machines apply forces and transfer energy, and all the steps that you designed work together to perform a task.

COUNTING ON CHEMICAL REACTIONS

Boom!

Fireworks are not just dazzling, explosive displays but also chemical reactions! The first fireworks were developed in ancient China more than 2,000 years ago. It all began when people burned bamboo stalks, which are hollow on the inside. As the stalks burned, the air inside overheated and exploded. At the time, they were called firecrackers and people thought they warded off evil spirits.

Several hundred years later, Chinese chemists mixed several substances that became the world's first gunpowder. The powder was poured into bamboo stalks. This created even more powerful and sparkling explosions. During the thirteenth century, fireworks spread to Europe and were used for celebrations. When settlers moved to North America, they brought fireworks with them and eventually it became a tradition to set them off on the Fourth of July.

With increasingly complex technology, chemists have further developed fireworks, mixing different chemicals for specific colors and displays.

Have you found yourself dreaming about building contraptions? Or thinking about building contraptions when you should be doing homework? Maybe you need to create a homework machine. Good luck!

Need ideas for your next contraption challenge? Check out these tips from Sprice Machine.

🔍 Sprice Machine tips

Most importantly, you've learned to think like an engineer and used your creativity and knowledge to brainstorm, test, and evaluate your contraptions. After tackling these last contraptions, perhaps you will take contraption building to a whole other level. Let your imagination run wild, have fun, and happy building!

ESSENTIAL QUESTION

How is energy used or released in chemical reactions?

ELEPHANT TOOTHPASTE

Let's kick off the challenges for this chapter with an extra fun, extra messy chemical reaction. No elephant required!

▸ **Challenge Identified.** Create a wacky contraption to produce a wacky chemical reaction! Design a contraption with at least five steps that include a chemical reaction and a wedge.

▸ **Brainstorm ideas and supplies.** For elephant toothpaste, see the step-by-step recipe. For the rest of the contraption, consider what to use for a wedge or how to make one. What other items do you want to use in your contraption?

▸ **Draw a plan.** Thinking backward, what steps do you want to take to add the yeast and water mixture to the hydrogen peroxide and soap mixture? Use everything you've learned so far to design this contraption.

▸ **Build.** Be sure to set up your chemical reaction in a tray to collect the toothpaste mess. Set up the other parts of the contraption and then combine the water and yeast last, so the mixture is ready to react with the hydrogen peroxide and soap.

How to Make Elephant Toothpaste

Gather the ingredients and supplies:

› a tray to catch the mess
› ½ cup hydrogen peroxide
› a plastic bottle
› a squirt of liquid dish soap
› food coloring (optional)
› 3 tablespoons of warm water
› 1 tablespoon dry yeast

Pour the ½ cup hydrogen peroxide into the plastic bottle and add a squirt of dish soap. Swirl to combine. If desired, add a few drops of food coloring.

In a measuring cup, place 3 tablespoons of warm tap water (it should not be too hot to touch). Add 1 tablespoon of dry yeast, mix together, and let sit for a minute.

Keep these two components separate until it's time to test your contraption!

> **Test.** Once the yeast and water mixture are in place, set off the chain reaction that (possibly) ends in a chemical reaction.

> **Evaluate.** Do you have elephant toothpaste all over the tray? If not, identify the problem. Did the parts of the contraption work as you planned? Did the chemical reaction take place? If not, consider the possible reasons for the lack of reaction. Were the amounts of the ingredients correct (more dish soap creates more bubbles)? Was the water warm enough to activate the yeast? (If the water was too hot, it may have killed off the yeast.) Pro tip: Try mixing a pinch of sugar with the water before adding the yeast.

> **Redesign.** If you redesign the contraption because you didn't end up with toothpaste, experiment with the chemical reaction first and then work backward with the other steps. Keep noodling on it and try again!

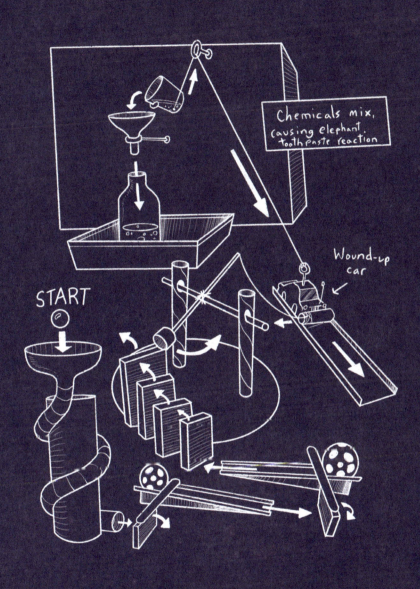

TEXT TO WORLD

What would dinner be like without any chemical reactions?

PAPER CLIP PET

Life is better with pets, so why not design a contraption that makes a pet—a paper clip pet, to be exact.

> **Watch this video by Sprice Machines to see how a chemical reaction was used in the middle of a wacky contraption.** What do you think they used to trigger that chemical reaction?
>
> 🔍 Sprice chemistry machine

▶ **Challenge Identified.** Incorporate a chemical reaction into the middle of your contraption to create a paper clip pet. Include a wedge, too.

▶ **Brainstorm ideas and supplies.** An example of a simple chemical reaction that you might want to incorporate involves using baking soda and vinegar to blow up a balloon. In addition to those three ingredients, you need a plastic bottle with a narrow opening. For the paper clip pet, you need paper clips, a strong magnet as the body of your pet to attract the clips, and eyes. Think about other objects (including a wedge) and steps to start this chain reaction and keep it going.

▶ **Draw a plan.** Consider starting by drawing the chemical reaction in the middle of the chain reaction and the paper clip pet at the end and then fill in all the other steps between, as well as at the beginning.

What's the Theme?

One thing to think about when building contraptions is using a theme. Advertisers are good at this—they use themes to sell products. The Honda contraption was made of car parts, the Target design was made entirely using food and kitchen items, and the Samsung ad had a travel theme.

Other possible themes to build your contraptions around:

birthdays	sports	seasons
holidays	nature	toys
school	colors	recycling
travel	instruments	cooking

> **Build.** As you assemble your contraption, be careful to keep the baking soda and vinegar separate.

> **Test.** Set off the chain reaction and step back!

> **Evaluate.** Look at the chemical reaction first. Was the combination of baking soda and vinegar correct? Also look at your pet—is it covered in paper clips? If not, what happened? Assess how your wedge performed, too, as well as all the other parts of the contraption.

> **Redesign.** If the chemical reaction didn't work, experiment a bit with baking soda and vinegar measurements and combinations before redesigning and rebuilding. Address other areas that did not transfer energy as expected, adjusting the amount of force or switching out or rearranging elements.

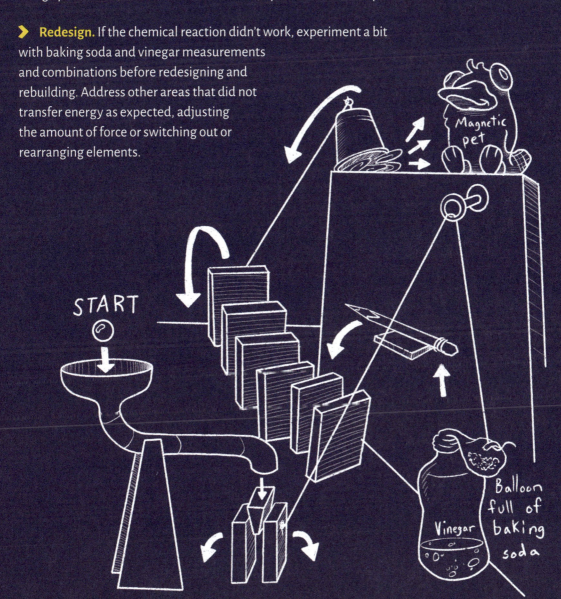

MAKE A **MUG CAKE**

Engineers need fuel to keep them going. Why not make yourself a little treat?

> **Challenge Identified.** Use as many different items as possible to make yourself a mug cake in 10 or more steps.

> **Brainstorm ideas and supplies.** By now, you've accumulated a lot of supplies and created many different contraptions. How can you put together everything you have learned to make a mug cake or pop a bag of popcorn? You need a microwave and either the ingredients for a mug cake or a bag of popcorn to cook.

> **Draw a plan.** Determine how your contraption can start the microwave and begin your drawing with this step. Look at the checklist below and consider how you can incorporate each of these in the contraption. If you make a mug cake, electricity and a chemical reaction are already included!

* Elastic potential energy
* Gears
* Magnets
* Water
* Electricity
* Chemical reaction
* Pulley
* Screw
* Inclined plane
* Lever
* Wedge
* Wheel and axle

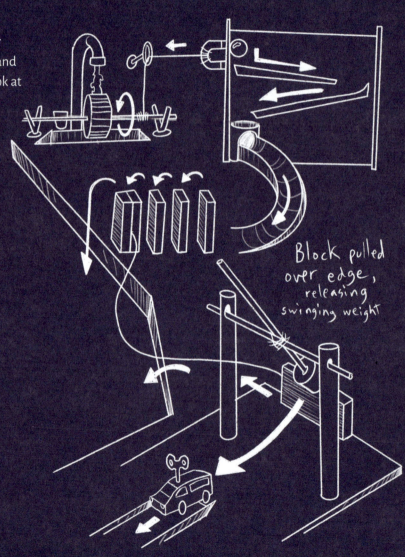

> **Build.** Follow your design to set up all the pieces and mix the cake ingredients.

> **Test.** Hungry? Let's cook!

> **Evaluate.** If you are eating the cake now, job well done. If not, never fear—you know what you need to do. Assess what worked and what didn't, consider where you had too much force or too little, and move on to redesigning.

> **Redesign.** Time to tinker with your design if you are not enjoying a snack just yet. Add or remove steps or think about how you could rearrange them.

Super Challenge

Look through your workshop and lay out all the items you've used and created in the previous challenges. Create a contraption of at least 25 steps that uses as many of those items as you can.

How to Make a Mug Cake

Ingredients:

- ½ tablespoon butter
- 3 tablespoons milk
- ¼ teaspoon vanilla
- 4 tablespoons all-purpose flour (or gluten-free flour)
- ½ teaspoon baking powder
- 2 teaspoons brown sugar
- pinch salt
- 2 tablespoons chocolate chips (optional, but highly recommended)

Put butter and milk in a 12- or 16-ounce microwavable coffee mug. Microwave for 30 seconds or until butter is melted (cover the cup so the butter doesn't splatter and make a mess).

Add the remaining ingredients. Stir until combined. Scrape down the sides of the mug.

Bake in the microwave for 45 to 60 seconds or until the batter is cooked through. (Different microwaves have different strengths, so you may need to experiment. Start with less time and then add time if needed.)

Let sit for a few minutes to cool. Eat and enjoy!

CRITTER **FEEDER**

Up to now, we have talked about energy transfers moving along a single path in your contraptions—one element to the next, to the next, and so on. But some energy transfers diverge! A good example is water from a burst pipe—the energy of the flowing water spurts out in many directions. Also, when electricity moves from the power plant through the wires, the energy diverges and goes to many different homes and businesses. **For this last contraption, the chain reaction should diverge at some point.**

> **Challenge Identified.** You are hereby challenged to make a chain reaction that diverges and then **reconverges** at least once. Your contraption should have a dozen or more steps and use as many of the elements you've learned about in this book as you can. Your goal is to launch seeds for the critters.

> **Brainstorm ideas and supplies.** Focus first on how you might diverge the chain reaction in your contraption. Dominoes can diverge and later reconverge. You could also send water down different paths and have it spill back into the same container. Or consider having marbles move in different directions and then reconverge so the collective energy of the marbles creates a force to keep the chain reaction going. Clearly, you need seeds. And what will launch them? If not seeds, what else could you launch . . . and clean up?

Bioluminescence

Have you ever watched fireflies blinking on a warm summer night or visited an aquarium and seen glowing animals in dark tanks? Then you have witnessed another type of chemical reaction in nature: **bioluminescence**. This is an **organism's** ability to produce and emit light. Animals use bioluminescence to find a mate, attract or sneak up on **prey**, or outwit prey and escape.

The light is produced by a chemical reaction between two substances, luciferin and luciferase, when they mix with oxygen. The chemical reaction releases energy in the form of light.

Some organisms produce these substances within their bodies, while others get them from the food they eat. Other species don't make light at all but rely on bioluminescent bacteria to make light for them. For example, the light in the lure dangling in front of a female anglerfish is not produced by her but by bioluminescent bacteria.

> **Draw a plan.** Use everything you've learned so far to design this last contraption. If you haven't done so before, consider adding arrows to your drawing that explain the transfer of energy and label the elements to your drawing.

> **Build.** First, get permission from an adult to launch seeds (or other material). Then, build this last, but ideally not final, contraption and prepare for launch.

> **Test.** Prepare for launch . . . Go!

> **Evaluate.** Was it easier or harder than expected to coordinate diverging and reconverging momentum? Evaluate the whole contraption—you know how to do this!

> **Redesign.** Rework your design to improve the diverging energy transfer. Or maybe you want to add steps to make the contraption even more complicated and ridiculous . . . because, in the end, that is what it's all about!

WORDS TO KNOW

diverge: to separate from the main path and go in another direction.

reconverge: to come together again.

bioluminescence: an organism's ability to produce and emit light.

organism: a living thing, such as a plant or animal.

prey: an animal hunted and eaten by other animals.

Super Challenge

Combine elastic potential energy, magnets, gears, belts, a motor, water, a chemical reaction, and all six simple machines in one contraption of at least 20 steps.

SHUT THE DOOR

Why just give a door a push to close it when you can create an overly complicated contraption to do the job?

> **Challenge Identified.** Transfer energy up and down three times each, in a contraption with 10 or more steps, to eventually close a door. You might consider short distances up and down, such as from the floor to a tabletop. Or you might challenge yourself to go up and down a flight of steps or to the top of a tall cabinet.

Super Superlatives

Time out now for a short language arts lesson about superlatives! A superlative is an adjective that describes something as the best or worst in quality. A contraption you built in the chemical reactions chapter could be described as the wackiest—or even the messiest. Or perhaps you had a contraption you could describe as the worst because so many elements failed.

Use superlatives to challenge yourself to come up with different contraptions. For example, how would you go about making the largest contraption yet? Think about the size of the elements and the space you need. Or maybe you do not have a lot of space, and you want to make the smallest machine you can—everything in miniature. There are so many ways to challenge yourself. Here are a few ideas.

Largest	Quietest	Neatest
Smallest	Loudest	Messiest
Slowest	Fastest	Tallest

Take a look at some of these superlative sensations!

Seiko smallest Goldberg

CNN slow Goldberg

largest Rube Goldberg

> **Brainstorm ideas and supplies.** Perhaps start by thinking about objects that can transfer energy upward. Here are some ideas that might help.

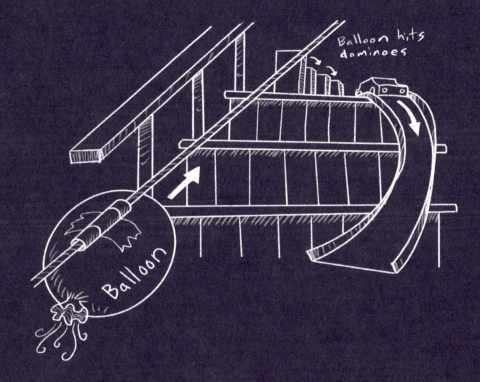

Use dominoes on stairs to move energy upward. You can use large dominoes made from building blocks, books, or cereal boxes to go up a set of stairs. Try a balloon zip line. With enough force, the elastic potential energy in an inflated balloon can zip upward and transfer energy to a higher location. Look at the challenge in the "Introduction" to remind yourself about the forces at work when you release air from a balloon. Configure pulleys (of any kind) and gears to move objects up and down. Use an electric motor to generate enough force to move an object such as an elevator upward. Use springs and rubber bands to launch objects upward. Include a strong magnet to pull up a metallic object. Naturally, you need a door. What will you use to close it—a push or pull?

> **Draw a plan.** Sketch out this door-closing machine, making sure that your energy transfers go up and down three times and that your contraption includes at least 10 steps.

> **Build.** Put it all together, linking steps carefully so the chain reaction doesn't stall.

> **Test.** Put your contraption to work.

> **Evaluate.** Were you successful at transferring energy up and down three times? Did your contraption have enough energy to maintain momentum throughout? Were there places without enough force to move objects upward? Did the door close?

> **Redesign.** If a step didn't work, consider replacing or modifying it in some way. Experiment more with forces transferring energy upwards. Redesign accordingly and try again!

GLOSSARY

adapter: a device for connecting two parts (as of different diameters) of an apparatus

air resistance: the force of air pushing against an object.

analog watch: a watch that shows the time using numbers around the edge and hands that point to the numbers.

apex: the highest point of something.

applied force: a force that is applied to an object by a person or another object.

aqueduct: a network of channels used to move water across long distances.

archaeological: having to do with archaeology, the study of ancient people through the objects they left behind.

atmosphere: the blanket of gases surrounding Earth.

atom: a small piece of matter made of protons and neutrons orbited by electrons.

attract: a force that pulls things closer.

axis: an imaginary line around which an object rotates.

battery: a device that produces an electric current using chemicals.

BCE: put after a date, BCE stands for Before Common Era and counts down to zero. CE stands for Common Era and counts up from zero. These non-religious terms correspond to BC and AD.

bioluminescence: an organism's ability to produce and emit light.

boiling point: the temperature at which a liquid boils.

bond: a force that holds together the atoms or groups of atoms in a molecule.

brainstorm: to think creatively and without judgment, often in a group of people.

cameo: a single, very brief appearance, especially by a famous person.

catapult: a device used to hurl or launch an object.

cell: the basic part of a living thing. Cells are so small they can be seen only with a microscope. There are billions of cells in most living things.

chain reaction: a series of events in which one action causes the next one and so on.

chemical energy: energy from a chemical reaction.

chemical reaction: the rearrangement of atoms in a substance to make a new chemical substance.

chemistry: the science of the properties of substances and how they interact, combine, and change.

chlorophyll: the chemical in a plant's cell that gives a plant its green color.

circuit: a complete path of an electrical current.

cog: the tooth on the rim of a wheel or gear.

collision: an event that occurs when a moving object bumps or crashes into another object.

compass: a device with a magnetic needle that points north.

compress: to squeeze or push a material with force.

condensation: the process of a gas cooling down and changing into a liquid.

conductor: a material through which electricity can move quickly and easily, which includes most metals.

continent: one of the earth's large landmasses, including Africa, Antarctica, Australia, North America, South America, and Asia and Europe (called Eurasia).

GLOSSARY

contraption: a machine or device that may seem unnecessarily complicated or strange.

convoluted: complex and difficult to follow.

corrode: to rust.

current: the flow of electricity.

debut: to introduce.

diameter: the distance across a circle through its middle.

discharge: the sudden flow of electrons from one object to another.

diverge: to separate from the main path and go in another direction.

drought: a long period of unusually low rainfall that can harm plants, animals, and humans.

ecosystem: a community of living and nonliving things and their environment.

elasticity: the ability of an object or material to return to its original shape after being compressed or stretched.

electric current: the flow of electricity.

electrical charge: a fundamental property of matter. Protons have a positive charge, electrons have a negative charge, and neutrons have no charge.

electrical force: the push or pull between two electrically charged objects.

electricity: a form of energy caused by the movement of tiny particles called electrons. It provides power for lights, appliances, video games, and many other electric devices.

electrode: a conductor through which electricity enters or leaves an object such as a battery.

electrolyte: in a battery, a gel or liquid that conducts electricity.

electromagnet: a magnet that uses electricity to create a magnetic field.

electron: a negatively charged particle that spins in an orbit around the nucleus in an atom.

emit: to send or give out something, such as smoke, gas, heat, or light.

energy: the ability to do work or cause change.

engineer: a person who uses science, math, and creativity to design and build things.

engineering design process: the series of steps that guides engineering teams as they solve problems.

ethylene: a gas produced by many fruits and vegetables that triggers ripening.

evaporation: the process of a liquid heating up and becoming a gas.

exert: to put forth effort or force.

expand: to spread out and take up more space.

fermentation: the chemical breakdown of substances by yeast, mold, or bacteria.

force: a push or pull that has the potential to change an object's motion.

fossil fuels: fuel made from the remains of plants and animals that lived millions of years ago. Coal, oil, and natural gas are fossil fuels.

friction: a force that slows a moving object or objects when they move against each other.

fulcrum: the fixed point on which a lever sits or is supported and on which it moves.

galvanized: coated with a layer of zinc.

gas: one of the three states of matter. The particles in a gas are not bound to each other and move very fast in all directions. A gas does not have a definite shape or volume.

GLOSSARY

gauss: the measurement of a magnet's strength.

gear: a wheel with teeth around the rim, used in objects to create a mechanical advantage.

gear train: a system of two or more interlocked gears that transmits motion from one gear to the next.

generator: a machine that converts energy to electricity.

glacier: a slowly moving mass of ice and snow.

gravitational potential energy: the energy stored in an object as the result of its height above Earth.

gravity: a force that pulls objects toward each other and all objects to the earth.

helium: a gas that's lighter than air.

hobbing machine: a special tool that cuts the cogs on gears.

horizontal: straight across from side to side.

hydrology: the study of water and how it moves in relation to the land.

hydropower: the energy produced by moving water.

indigenous: native to a certain location or area.

Industrial Revolution: a period during the eighteenth and nineteenth centuries when large-scale production of goods began and large cities and factories began to replace small towns and farming.

input force: the force applied to make an object move.

insulator: a material such as plastic or rubber that does not allow electricity to pass through easily or at all.

interlock: to firmly join together, with one part fitting into another.

kinetic energy: the energy an object possesses when it is in motion.

latex: a substance from which rubber can be made, found in more than 2,000 plant species, including rubber trees.

levitate: to rise and hover in the air.

linear force: a force applied along a straight line.

liquid: one of the three states of matter. The particles in a liquid cluster together and flow. A liquid takes the shape of its container.

load: something that is carried or moved, especially something heavy.

lock: on a river or canal, a system for raising and lowering boats.

lodestone: a naturally occurring mineral with magnetic properties.

maglev: a transportation system where trains glide above a track using the power of magnets.

magnet: a special kind of rock or metal that attracts certain metals.

magnetic field: the area around a magnet in which its magnetic force is felt.

magnetic force: a force that occurs when the poles of a magnet interact.

magnetism: a force that creates a push or a pull on magnetic objects.

magnetize: to make magnetic.

mass: the amount of matter or stuff in something. On Earth, the mass of something is very close to its weight.

matter: any material or substance that has mass and takes up space.

mechanical advantage: the benefit gained by using a machine to do work with less effort.

GLOSSARY

medical resonance imaging (MRI): a medical test that produces detailed images of the inside of the human body.

Mesoamerica: the region that includes parts of Mexico and Central America.

migration: the movement of a large group of animals, such as birds, due to changes in the environment.

mineral: a naturally occurring solid found in rocks and in the ground. Rocks are made of minerals. Gold and diamonds are precious minerals.

molecule: a group of atoms bonded together, the simplest structural unit of an element or compound. Molecules can break apart and form new ones, which is a chemical reaction.

momentum: a measure of a mass in motion.

nanometer: a very small unit of measurement, just one-billionth of a meter.

navigation: planning and following a route.

neutron: a particle in the nucleus of an atom that does not have a charge.

newton (N): the unit used to measure force.

nonlinear: not in a straight line.

nucleus: the center of an atom, which contains protons and neutrons

orbit: the path of an object circling another object.

organ: a part of the body with a special function, such as the heart, lungs, brain, and skin.

organism: a living thing, such as a plant or animal.

output force: the amount of force exerted on an object by a simple machine.

oxidation: the loss or transfer of electrons.

patent: the rights granted to an inventor for their invention so others may not copy or take advantage of it.

photosynthesis: the process through which plants use water, carbon dioxide, and sunlight to make their food.

physics: the science of how matter and energy work together.

pivot: to turn or move on a fixed spot.

plasticity: the ability of an object or material to be permanently molded or shaped.

pole: on a magnet, the north or south end where the magnetic field is strongest.

potential energy: the energy stored inside an object when it is still or at rest.

precipitation: water that falls to the ground in the form of rain, snow, sleet, or hail.

prey: an animal hunted and eaten by other animals.

product: the new substance created when two or more substances are combined.

proton: a positively charged particle located in the nucleus of an atom.

rack and pinion gear: a gear that consists of a toothed rod (the rack) and a circular gear that runs along the rod (the pinion gear).

reactant: a substance being changed in a chemical reaction.

reconverge: to come together again.

Renaissance: a cultural movement or rebirth that took place in Europe from the fourteenth through the seventeenth centuries.

renewable energy: power that comes from sources that will not run out, such as water, wind, and sun.

repel: to push away.

GLOSSARY

resistance band: a large elastic band used for strength training.

ricochet: to rebound one or more times off a surface.

rotational force: a force that causes an object to rotate around a fixed axis.

shaft: a bar that connects one gear to another and transfers power from one to the other.

simple machine: a mechanical device that changes the direction or magnitude of a force. The six simple machines are the lever, inclined plane, wheel and axle, pulley, screw, and wedge..

slapstick: comedy stressing ridiculous situations and horseplay.

solid: one of the three states of matter. The particles of a solid are bound tightly. A solid has a definite shape and volume and does not flow.

species: a group of living things that are closely related and can produce young.

spring force: a restoring force found in elastic materials that makes the material stretch or compress and then return to its original position when released.

static electricity: an imbalance of electrical charges caused by transferring electrons from one object to another.

steam engine: an engine that burns wood or coal to heat water and create steam. The steam generates power to run the engine.

stored potential energy: stored energy in an elastic material that results from stretching or compressing.

sustainable: being used without being completely used up or destroyed.

synchronized: working together at the same time or rate.

synthetic: produced artificially to imitate a natural product.

technology: tools, methods, and systems used to solve a problem or do work.

tension: a pulling force that pulls or stretches an object.

terrain: land or ground and all of its physical features, such as hills, rocks, and water.

thread: the raised edge of a screw that winds around.

trial and error: trying first one thing, then another and another, until something works.

turbine: a machine that harnesses the kinetic energy of moving liquids or gases to turn a wheel and generate power.

universe: everything that exists everywhere.

vapor: a substance suspended in the air as a gas, such as steam, mist, or fog.

vertical: straight up and down.

vibrate: to move back and forth or side to side very quickly.

volt (V): the unit used to measure the electric potential between two spots in a circuit.

voltage: the force of an electric current, measured in volts.

volume: the amount of space occupied by something.

water cycle: the continuous movement of water on Earth through the processes of precipitation, evaporation, and condensation.

work: the amount of energy needed to move an object a certain distance.

RESOURCES

POSSIBLE TASKS OR CHALLENGES

- Knock something over
- Ring a bell
- Pop a balloon
- Open/close a door
- Raise a flag
- Open/shut a window
- Pull curtains open/closed
- Roll a dice
- Swat a fly
- Trap a leprechaun or mouse
- Rattle a wind chime
- Switch on/off a light
- Hit an easy button
- Knock a bone off a table for the dog
- Launch a dog treat
- Water a plant
- Plant seeds in a pot
- Destroy a house of cards
- Squeeze toothpaste onto a brush
- Close a book
- Turn a page in a book
- Toss a gum wrapper in the trash
- Play with the cat
- Deliver a note
- Deliver a cookie or candy
- Zip a zipper
- Bother a sibling
- Apply a Band-Aid
- Wake up the dog
- Dispense a drop of soap
- Bang a drum
- Open an umbrella
- Make tea/dunk a tea bag
- Turn on a CD player
- Display a message/memo
- Score a goal/basket
- Put a stamp on a letter
- Trap a toy monster
- Turn on/off a fan
- Sail a boat across a "pond"
- Screw in a lightbulb
- Tighten the lid on a jar or bottle
- Staple papers together
- Feed the dog (or whatever pet you have!)

RESOURCES

- Turn on/off a water faucet
- Erase a chalkboard
- Put coins in a piggy bank
- Pour a bowl of cereal
- Bowl a strike
- Collapse a tower or pyramid
- Toss a ball
- Spin a whirligig
- Pop a fake snake in a can
- Launch a marshmallow
- Use a slingshot
- Pour a soda
- Launch a parachute
- Make a sandwich
- Make lemonade
- Play drums/xylophone
- Make a splash-paint painting
- Make a volcano erupt
- Put out a candle
- Launch a rocket
- "Sprout" flowers
- Launch confetti
- Make it snow
- Make a marionette/puppet show
- Launch a paper airplane
- Make popcorn

TOP EIGHT HANDY SUPPLIES

- Glue gun (and glue sticks!)
- Tape
- Dominoes
- Empty toilet paper rolls
- Empty paper towel tubes
- Popsicle sticks
- Rubber bands
- Magnets

RESOURCES

HANDY TOYS

- Marbles
- Balls
- Tennis balls
- Softballs
- Baseballs
- Bowling balls
- Toy cars
- Car tracks
- Skateboard
- Roller skates
- Golf balls

- Ping-pong balls
- Toy trains
- Wooden blocks
- Dominoes
- Legos
- Toy trains
- Toy train tracks
- Marble runs
- Action figures
- Stuffed animals

HANDY ART SUPPLIES

- Graph paper
- String
- Yarn
- Tape
- Pins
- Popsicle sticks
- Pencils

- Binder clips
- Scissors
- Glue gun (and glue sticks!)
- Tape
- Pipe cleaners
- Construction paper

RESOURCES

RECYCLABLES

- Cereal boxes
- Plastic water bottles and caps
- Cans
- Aluminum foil
- Plastic containers
- Cardboard
- Toilet paper and paper towel rolls
- Lids

MISCELLANEOUS

- Clothespins
- Chopsticks
- Straws
- Toothpicks
- Bowls
- Hammer
- Balloons
- Funnel
- Bucket
- Cups and bowls
- Straws
- Trays
- Pieces of wood
- PVC pipe
- Plastic tubing
- Gutters
- Plastic spoons
- Rope
- Pulley
- Peg board
- Thread spools
- Ribbon spools

RESOURCES

SELECTED BIBLIOGRAPHY

education.nationalgeographic.org/resource/isaac-newton-who-he-was-why-apples-are-falling

physicsclassroom.com/class/newtlaws

rubegoldberg.org/all-about-rube/cartoon-gallery

eia.gov/kids/what-is-energy/forms-of-energy.

solarschools.net/knowledge-bank/energy/types

energyeducation.ca/encyclopedia/elastic_potential_energy

scientificamerican.com/article/bring-science-home-rubber-bands-energy

wonderopolis.org/wonder/how-were-rubber-bands-invented

thoughtco.com/magnets-and-metals-2340001

teachengineering.org

americanscientist.org/article/gears-drive-the-world

khkgears.net/new/gear_knowledge/introduction_to_gears

europeansprings.com/the-use-of-springs-in-toys

noaa.gov/education/resource-collections/freshwater/water-cycle

nps.gov/articles/000/the-power-of-water-creating-energy

Metric Conversions

Use this chart to find the metric equivalents to the English measurements in this book. If you need to know a half measurement, divide by two. If you need to know twice the measurement, multiply by two. How do you find a quarter measurement? How do you find three times the measurement?

English	Metric
1 inch	2.5 centimeters
1 foot	30.5 centimeters
1 yard	0.9 meter
1 mile	1.6 kilometers
1 pound	0.5 kilogram
1 teaspoon	5 milliliters
1 tablespoon	15 milliliters
1 cup	237 milliliters

RESOURCES

ESSENTIAL QUESTIONS

Introduction: How does designing and building wacky contraptions use engineering principles?

Chapter 1: How can you use the elastic potential energy in springs and rubber bands to do work?

Chapter 2: How can you use the pushing and pulling forces of a magnet to change the direction and speed of a moving object?

Chapter 3: How do gears increase the speed or change the direction of an input force?

Chapter 4: How can water be used to generate energy?

Chapter 5: What is electricity and how can we harness it to do work and power wacky contraptions?

Chapter 6: How is energy used or released in chemical reactions?

BOOKS

Blobaum, Cindy. *Gravity: Mass, Energy, and the Force that Holds Things Together with Hands-On Science Activities for Kids.* Nomad Press, 2023.

George, Jennifer, and Zach Umperovitch. *Rube Goldberg's Big Book of Building: Make 25 Machines That Really Work!* Harry N. Abrams, 2024.

Gifford, Clive. *How Everything Works.* Lonely Planet, 2022.

Macaulay, David. *The Way Things Work: Newly Revised Edition: The Ultimate Guide to How Things Work.* Clarion Books, 2023.

Perdew, Laura. *Crazy Contraptions: Build Rube Goldberg Machines that Swoop, Spin, Stack, and Swivel with Engineering Activities.* Nomad Press, 2019.

Snider, Brandon T. *Rube Goldberg and His Amazing Machines.* Harry N. Abrams, 2022.

Van Vleet, Carmella. *Electricity: Circuits, Static, and Electromagnets with Hands-On Science Activities for Kids.* Nomad Press, 2022.

WEBSITES

STEM Inventions: *stem-inventions.com/projects*

Inventors of Tomorrow: *inventorsoftomorrow.com*

Exploratorium Cranky Contraptions: *exploratorium.edu tinkering/projects/cranky-contraption-explorations*

Wonderopolis: *wonderopolis.org/wonder/what-is-a-rube-goldberg-machine*

Connections Academy: *connectionsacademy.com/support/resourcesarticle/build-your-own-rube-goldberg-machine*

RESOURCES

QR CODE GLOSSARY

Page 2: pbs.org/video/newtons-laws-ojfyy9

Page 7: rubegoldberg.org/all-about-rube/a-cultural-icon

Page 11: nhpbs.pbslearningmedia.org/resource/idptv11.sci.phys.maf.d4ksim/simple-machines

Page 16: nhpbs.pbslearningmedia.org/resource/hew06.sci.phys.maf.rollercoaster/energy-in-a-roller-coaster-ride

Page 19: youtube.com/watch?v=ZG2XJut8TeU

Page 20: eia.gov/kids

Page 22: ctsciencecenter.org/blog/science-at-play-rube-goldberg-machines

Page 27: instructables.com/how-to-make-a-desktop-catapult

Page 31: youtube.com/watch?v=r8d1g_YCrE4&t=175s

Page 33: youtube.com/watch?v=8os4A4li674

Page 34: kids.kiddle.co/earth%27s_magnetic_field

Page 36: youtube.com/watch?v=atK4irkgm_U

Page 36: youtube.com/watch?v=l7cFpRsTz3k

Page 36: youtube.com/watch?v=6-TG6SNNL6I

Page 36: youtube.com/watch?v=_ve4M4UsJQo

Page 36: youtube.com/watch?v=pSjSIdqK_wk

Page 38: ed.ted.com/best_of_web/iUTasbff

Page 40: youtube.com/watch?v=O33Av6AXb0Q

Page 42: foldnfly.com/#/1-1-1-1-1-1-1-1-2-1

Page 45: youtube.com/watch?v=odpsm3yhPsA

Page 46: thekidshouldseethis.com/post/how-do-bike-gears-work-video

Page 47: youtube.com/watch?v=5hKTvVG6eqA

Page 49: thekidshouldseethis.com/post/gear-shapes-square-oval-pentagonal-video

Page 51: thekidshouldseethis.com/post/red-ball-adventure-a-chain-reaction-marble-run-on-a-pegboard-wall

Page 53: youtube.com/watch?v=_8_n3uDUqd4

Page 57: thekidshouldseethis.com/post/how-does-a-wind-up-music-box-work

Page 60: youtube.com/watch?v=PDbJPK-GI3k

Page 61: amnh.org/explore/ology/water/what-is-water

Page 62: thekidshouldseethis.com/post/pass-the-salt-an-intricate-food-themed-rube-goldberg-machine

Page 67: littlebinsforlittlehands.com/how-to-make-a-water-wheel

Page 67: youtube.com/watch?v=ziU6Krb3YiE

RESOURCES

QR CODE GLOSSARY (CONT.)

Page 67: education.com/science-fair/article/water-produce-energy

Page 74: okgosandbox.org/this-too-shall-pass

Page 76: thinktv.pbslearningmedia.org/resource/phy03.sci.phys.mfe.zsnap/static-electricity-snap-crackle-jump

Page 78: stemgeneration.org/potato-power

Page 79: acs.org/education/celebrating-chemistry-editions/2024-ccew/on-the-hunt-for-batteries.html

Page 80: ed.ted.com/lessons/why-batteries-die-adam-jacobson

Page 85: nhpbs.pbslearningmedia.org/resource/phy03.sci.phys.energy.zmilk/building-simple-machines-a-glass-of-milk-please/#.WpM822Y-LdQ

Page 86: youtube.com/watch?v=KxlLxMYYMYk

Page 90: youtube.com/watch?v=jzjBAAv9nxc

Page 92: ted.com/talks/stephanie_warren_the_chemistry_of_cookies

Page 93: bartonhillfarms.com/photosynthesis-for-kids

Page 95: pbs.org/video/its-okay-be-smart-six-reactions

Page 97: youtube.com/watch?v=p8Wwq_B5S7I

Page 100: youtube.com/watch?v=-ICgcxQt_mA

Page 106: youtube.com/watch?v=cSg-yFZ7y0A

Page 106: youtube.com/watch?v=8hGR45yiv8c

Page 106: youtube.com/watch?v=VpLDfkLBJ0Q

INDEX

A

activities
- Apply a Bandage, 84–85
- Balloons and the Laws of Motion, 13
- Bowl a Strike, 68–69
- Close a Box, 52–53
- Critter Feeder, 104–105
- Deliver a Message, 70–71
- Demolition by Slingshot, 24–25
- Elephant Toothpaste, 98–99
- GOOOOAL!, 40–41
- Make a Mug Cake, 102–103
- Marshmallow Launcher, 26–27
- Move a Giraffe, 54–55
- Open a Happy-Face-in-the-Box, 56–57
- Paper Airline Launcher, 42–43
- Paper Clip Pet, 100–101
- Pop a Balloon, 86–87
- Pour a Bowl of Cereal, 66–67
- Ring a Bell, 38–39
- Shut the Door, 106–107
- Spring Sprouts, 23
- Turn on a Light, 83

aqueducts, 35, 37
Archimedes's screw, 82
Aristotle, 48
atoms, 72–73, 91

INDEX

B
batteries, 19, 76–82, 92
Benigno, Alex, 38
bicycles, 38, 44–47
bioluminescence, 104
boats and ships, 61–62

C
catapults, 18, 26–27
chain reactions
  chemical reactions creating, 92, 95
  contraptions with, 1, 17, 36, 43, 64, 74. *See also* activities
  energy for, 8–9, 14
  Goldberg using, 7. *See also* Rube Goldberg machines
chemical reactions, 88–107
  in batteries, 78–79
  in bioluminescence, 104
  contraptions with, 98–103
  description of, 88–89
  energy and, 78–79, 92
  everyday, 92–93
  experiments with, 95
  in fireworks, 97
  historical impacts of, 95
  matter and, 90–91
  in photosynthesis, 93
  warning for safety with, 94
  wedges and, 96–97
Cochrane, Josephine, 65
collisions, 47
compasses, 29, 32–33
contraptions. *See also* Rube Goldberg machines
  building of, 11–12. *See also* activities
  chemical reactions in. *See also* chemical reactions
  electricity in. *See also* electricity
  engineering design process for, 2, 5
  forces affecting, 2–4
  gears in. *See also* gears
  ideas for, 97. *See also* activities
  laws of motion for, 2, 4–8, 13
  magnets in. *See also* magnets
  simple machines in. *See also* simple machines
  tension in. *See also* tension
  themes for, 100
  water in. *See also* water

D
da Vinci, Leonardo, 46
dishwashers, 65

E
Earth's magnetic field, 32–33, 34, 35
elasticity
  plasticity vs., 20
  as potential energy, 17–20, 24–27, 42, 50, 57
electricity, 72–87
  batteries and, 76–82. *See also* batteries
  contraptions with, 82–87
  description of, 72–73
  electric current or circuit in, 73, 76–81, 86, 104
  forces with, 4
  hydropower creating, 60–61, 63, 64
  magnets and, 30, 34
  power sources for, 77–78, 79
  screws and, 81–87
  speed of, 84
  static, 74–76, 77
  voltage of, 78, 80
  warning on dangers of, 81
energy
  chemical, 78–79, 92
  electric. *See also* electricity
  kinetic. *See also* kinetic energy
  potential. *See also* potential energy
  steam, 58, 62–63, 78
  transfers of, 8–9, 31, 47, 51, 60, 104, 106–107
  water-based (hydro), 60–61, 63, 64, 66–67, 104
  work and, 8–9
engineering
  careers in, 10
  design process in, 2, 5

F
films, contraptions in, 17, 85
fireworks, 97
forces, 2–4
friction, 4, 5, 74–75
fruit, ripening of, 89, 90

G
gases, 58–59, 90. *See also* steam
gears, 44–57
  contraptions with, 52–57
  description of, 44
  history of, 48–49
  physics of, 45–47
  uses of, 49–50, 57
  wheels, axles and, 44, 50–54
Goldberg, Rube, 7, 85. *See also* Rube Goldberg machines
gravity, 3, 5, 15–16, 25

H
hobbing machines, 48–49
hydropower and hydroelectric energy, 60–61, 63, 64, 66–67, 104

I
inclined planes, iv, v, 35–39, 81. *See also* screws

J
jack-in-the-box, 53

K
kinetic energy
  conversion to, 15–17, 19, 25, 50, 78
  description of, 9, 14–15
  electricity as, 73, 76. *See also* electricity
  transfers of, 9, 31, 60
  water-based, 60, 63. *See also* hydropower and hydroelectric energy

INDEX

L

laws of motion, 2, 4–8, 13
levers, iv, 21–22, 26–27
liquids, 58–59, 89, 90. *See also* water
locks, water in, 61–62

M

magnets, 28–43
  in compasses, 29, 32–33
  contraptions with, 38–43
  description of, 28–29
  Earth as, 32–33, 34, 35
  forces with, 4, 30
  history of, 29, 31
  how magnets work, 30–32
  inclined planes and, 35–39
  measuring strength of, 35
  poles of, 31, 32
  in trains, 33
  uses of, 34, 36
matter, 90–91
motors, 30
music boxes, 57

N

Newton, Isaac, 3. *See also* laws of motion

O

OK Go, 74

P

photosynthesis, 93
plasticity, 20
potato batteries, 78
potential energy
  batteries with, 76, 79, 92
  chemical, 79, 92
  description of, 9, 14–15
  elastic, 17–20, 24–27, 42, 50, 57
  gravitational, 15–16, 25
  stored, 17, 25, 57, 63, 76
  transfers of, 31
  water-based, 63
pullback cars, 50
pulleys, v, 64–65, 67–71

R

Red Ball Adventure contraption, 51
roller coasters, 16
rubber and rubber bands, 17–19, 24–27, 42–43
Rube Goldberg machines. *See also* contraptions
  advertisements using, 36
  design contests for, 9
  films and videos of, 17, 22, 53, 62, 74, 85, 106
  games with, 69
  superlative, 106

S

screws, v, 81–87
simple machines
  description of, iv–v, 9–11
  inclined planes as, iv, v, 35–39, 81. *See also* screws
  levers as, iv, 21–22, 26–27
  pulleys as, v, 64–65, 67–71
  screws as, v, 81–87
  wedges as, v, 96–97
  wheels and axles as, iv, v, 44, 50–54, 64. *See also* gears; pulleys
slingshots, 18, 24–25
solids, 58–59, 89, 90
speed
  of electricity, 84
  laws of motion on, 6
springs, 4, 17, 19–20, 23, 25–27, 50, 57
stage rigging, 67
static electricity, 74–76, 77
steam, 58–59, 62–63, 78
superlatives, 106

T

tension, 14–27
  compression and, 17, 19, 23
  energy and, 14–20, 24–27
  as force, 4
  levers and, 21–22, 26–27
trains, 33, 62
trampolines, 25

V

voltage, 78, 80

W

water, 58–71
  contraptions with, 1, 66–71
  description of, 58–60
  energy or hydropower from, 60–61, 63, 64, 66–67, 104
  magnets in, 31
  pulleys and, 64–65, 68–71
  screws to move, 82
  states of, 58–59, 89, 90. *See also* steam
  steam from, 58–59, 62–63, 78
  uses of, 58, 60–62
  water cycle of, 59
wedges, v, 96–97
wheels and axles, iv, v, 44, 50–54, 64. *See also* gears; pulleys
work and energy, 8–9